A Time for Transformation

Also by Diana Cooper
LIGHT UP YOUR LIFE

DIANA COOPER

A Time for
Transformation

Empowering Your Life
Through Awareness

ASHGROVE PRESS, BATH

First published in Great Britain by
ASHGROVE PRESS LIMITED
4 Brassmill Centre, Brassmill Lane
Bath, Avon, BA1 3JN
and distributed in the USA by
Avery Publishing Group Inc.
120 Old Broadway, Garden City Park,
New York 11040

ISBN 1-85398-041-2

First published 1992

Photoset in 11/12½ pt Palatino by
Ann Buchan (Typesetters), Middlesex
Printed and bound in Great Britain by
Dotesios, Trowbridge,
Wiltshire

To my parents,
George and Aileen,
with love

CONTENTS

ONE

A Leopard Can Change His Spots

When I first saw Debbie, she looked square. She had a square jaw, a square face and she was solid. She was a policewoman.

Inside that solid, heavy, authoritarian person stood a soft, gentle, spiritual, very psychically sensitive woman, who gradually began to emerge as we worked together.

Debbie had been visiting a psychic for consultations every six months over a number of years. After she had been seeing me and working on herself for a few months, her next appointment with her psychic came round.

Debbie didn't tell the psychic that she had been in therapy and when she tuned in, the psychic couldn't believe it.

'What's happened to you isn't possible,' she said. 'You've totally changed your aura. You've changed your karma. You've changed your future. I've never seen anything like it. How have you done this?'

Debbie chuckled and thought of our sessions but wouldn't tell her. Now, some years later, after exploring her own Path, Debbie is no longer a policewoman. She is a very spiritual practising psychic herself.

As a child I was often told to be wary of people, because a leopard doesn't change his spots. Thankfully human beings are not leopards. I only have to think of Debbie to remind myself.

When we make a shift in consciousness we change our thoughts, our behaviour, our health, our karma and our future. We all have the possibility of total transformation and awakening to our soul's purpose.

Many of us spend our lives in a soul sleep of ignorance. When we are ready to step on the Path of Light, our Higher Self will try to wake us up. Often a trauma is the only way to shake usfully awake.

Yet it isn't necessary to wake in this painful way. Many of us put ourselves through trauma because we won't listen to our inner voice. So we create pain to force ourselves to look inside.

The commonest questions I am asked when people have read my first book *Light Up Your Life* are, 'How did you get into this work? Have you always known these things? Have you always been spiritual?'

The answer is No. I spent my first forty-two years in soul sleep. I did try to open up briefly once but it was too difficult and I closed down again until my life fell apart. I moved to England after years abroad. My marriage was breaking up. My children were put into boarding school.

I felt powerless and helpless and unsupported as if I'd fallen into a black hole. Somehow I had to find the strength to leave my husband, find a new home and find a way to earn a living. Everything seemed black despair. It was in this state of darkness that I threw myself into a chair one afternoon and said defiantly. 'If there is anything out there, show me.' I added sulkily (and arrogantly!) 'I've got one hour.'

I fell into a deep trance and a golden being appeared and took me out of my body into other planes of existence. At one point we were flying over a hall full of people covered in rainbow coloured auras. I said to the being, 'Am I down there in the audience.' He said, 'No you are on the platform. You are a teacher.' On the platform were transparent beings with rays of light flowing through them. He then took me further to show me other incredible sights.

When I opened my eyes it was exactly one hour later and I knew something profound had happened. It still took time and pain to make a new life but that experience set me on my Path of Light.

The Piscean Age has passed. We are now well into the

Aquarian Age, which is the Age of Enlightenment. This is the age in which we have the opportunity to find enlightenment, in otherwords to become conscious beings who can see the perfection in all things and wake to the Truth.

Opportunities are now being presented to help people wake up. We don't have to wake through pain. We can wake through joy. This book is one such catalyst to the Light.

TWO

The Golden Ray

Everything we send out comes back to us. Sometimes it takes along time to come back – maybe a lifetime or more.

One of the reasons it takes so long is this. If we send out anger, for example, the other person may absorb it like a sponge. A sponge will soak up poison and won't release it until it is squeezed. By Spiritual Law the poison will then be returned to its origional owner.

If we refuse to accept the anger or to soak up the poison, it returns immediately back to the person who sent it.

I was told this story by a friend. Her friend Clementine was living in a beautiful cottage in a small village. One day there was a knock on the door and a lady who had just moved into ahouse on the outskirts of the village stood there. Without preamble, she declared that she wanted to buy Clementine's cottage and asked her how much she would sell for.

Clementine was considerably taken aback and replied that her house was not for sale. She was adamant and the new villager left, muttering darkly.

Clementine felt uneasy. Her unease turned to concern and then to alarm as strange, nasty things started happening to and around her. She told a friend about her concerns and suspicions. Her friend took her to see an elderly psychic. This old man listened to Clementine's story gravely. Then he advised her to imagine herself holding a mirror up between herself and her possible enemy.

He explained that if the lady was sending Clementine destructive thoughts, Clementine would no longer absorb them, so allowing them to create havoc in her life. Instead the destructive thoughts would bounce off the mirror straight back to whoever sent them.

If the villager was not sending her destructive energy, then of course nothing would happen.

Clementine did exactly as she had been instructed and was shocked when less than a week later, the villager's house caught fire and burnt to the ground. She felt awed and somewhat guilty. In fact there was no need to feel guilt. The Law says, As you sow shall you reap. Her positive intervention had merely speeded up the process of karma.

To visualize holding up a mirror to bounce thoughts back to their owner is a very powerful technique.

There is, however, a more spiritual and equally effective way of handling negative thoughts sent to us. Just imagine your heart centre wide open so that the Love and Wisdom of the Universe is able to flow into you and all around you, cocooning you in golden energy. This golden energy of Love and Wisdom is the most powerful energy of all.

When the dark thought forms come towards us, we can dissolve them in the golden light and ask that golden balls of Love and Wisdom be directed back to the sender instead.

This makes us feel good; the person who has sent out destruction and received back love, feels good and his or her karma is transmuted by our love.

By this method the vast cloud of collective karma in the Universe can be dissolved.

If Clementine had put her heart into this technique, instead of merely protecting herself, the villager would have felt better. Her house would not have burnt down and there would have been more love in the Universe.

Remember: there is nothing to fear but fear itself.

The golden ray is very special and very powerful. It contains the essence of Universal energy, love and wisdom. It also has a gentleness about it which can be felt but which is difficult to explain. It is the colour ray most often used when we are musing and available to higher awareness.

Whenever I talk about the golden energy someone

invariably shares an experience they have had.

Jenny told me of her great dilemma. She didn't know if she loved her boyfriend enough to marry him. What if it was wrong and she was making a ghastly error? She churned the problem over and over for days and weeks.

Then one day she was sitting on a train and her mind became lulled. It is at these moments that we are receptive. Suddenly a golden light filled her heart and she *knew* that her boyfriend was the right person.

This is why it is so important to find our inner stillness. It is into this stillness, this silence within, that the Deep Wisdom can enter.

Many people find that they can make a deeper connection with this inner silence when they are out in nature. Nature doesn't judge like people do. Because of this, when we are with people our defences are up. And when we feel safe in the non-judgement of nature, then we can relax and hear the wisdom of our inner silence.

If we can't physically be out in nature it helps tremendously to imagine ourselves in a place of beauty and serenity.

Peter had had arthritis in his right knee for years. His job entailed bending and kneeling and his knee was painful and stiff. A doctor told him that he'd just have to take painkillers every day for the rest of his life. He believed this and kept going on aspirin.

Then he went on a weekend workshop where he got in touch with the anger he repressed about his father. During the weekend, he beat the anger out into a cushion, he shouted and he expressed all the emotions towards him that he'd never dared express in life. Next day he lay in bed and a gold light came into his leg and up his body. It entered his knee and healed it completely of arthritis. He hasn't had a twinge since.

We don't have to wait for the golden ray to come to us. We can open ourselves up to the energy by intent or visualisation and radiate it to do its magic.

Anita had been to one of my workshops where we talked about the golden ray of energy. She thought it was decidedly suspect and probably only worked for suggestible people – and, she persuaded herself, she was down to earth and pragmatic.

Some time later she had to go to a social event. Her ex-husband was to be there, as well as a couple who had been friends of both of theirs. However, when she had left her husband, this couple had sided with him. They supported him, visited him and refused to acknowledge Anita at all when they met.

The social event appeared a gloomy prospect but suddenly Anita remembered the golden energy. She opened her heart centre and visualised golden light flooding her body and creating a golden aura around her. She imagined herself protected by this and full of love. Then she set off to the social event, determined to be warm, friendly and golden.

She mixed with people she knew and didn't find herself in the company of her two ex-friends, but just kept herself golden and radiating love. Later in the evening, separately, the husband and wife came over to her and spoke civilly to her. They each said they were sorry they'd been unkind and judgemental. They would like to be friends again.

Anita was delighted and amazed. Her intellectual mind had difficulty in accepting the power of the golden vibration of love, but now that she had experienced it working, she said she would never doubt it again. Golden energy raises the consciousness of sender and receiver. It creates miracles. When we focus on the best in others, astonishing things happen.

Phillipa phoned me in despair one morning. Her teenage daughter was being rude and difficult. She was incredibly untidy and refusing to do anything to help at home. Phillipa was a single parent and had struggled to bring Ann up. She worked tremendously hard to pay her mortgage and support the two of them, so she had little time for social life. Not surprisingly her relationships with men were unsatisfactory. And she had no time or energy for her daughter.

I knew that Phillipa was getting no emotional nourishment herself, so how could she possibly nourish her daughter? Instead she bombarded Ann with resentful thoughts and unspoken demands. Ann picked these up, put up her defences and attacked her mother where it hurt, by being rude and difficult, untidy and unhelpful. Hence the telephone cry for help that morning.

The one thing that Phillipa could change and change quickly was her thought pattern towards Ann. I suggested that she set aside two twenty minute periods that day to focus on Ann with love. In that time she was to think about all the good things they'd done together, to remember all the nice qualities she had and then to hold her in golden light. Phillipa promised to do so.

She phoned me next day in a state of excitement and shock. She did exactly as I suggested during that day. When she arrived home she found that Ann had cleaned the kitchen and cooked her mother a special meal.

When Phillipa raised her consciousness and radiated the golden energy of love to her daughter, Ann had felt it and responded to it with love.

We are as powerful as that. Love is as powerful as that. We can light up the good in others as easily as that. We can light up ourselves as quickly as that.

We think it is such hard work to clear out the darkness within us. *It takes but a moment to switch on the light.*

THREE

Prosperity

Can you imagine a father wanting his child to be poor or unsuccessful? Can you imagine the richest, most generous, most loving Father of the Universe wanting his child to be anything other than totally happy and prosperous?

As an ordinary human loving parent I want the best for my children. It is my pleasure and delight to give to them because I love them. I would feel quite upset if they wouldn't accept a present because they didn't feel they deserved it. I would hope they knew I loved them because they are my children. I know they are only doing whatever they are doing because that is their way of learning lessons.

Yet we often act as if we don't deserve anything from the Universal Father. We act as if we expect Him to be mingy and stingy. We cheat and lie and beg and steal rather than ask, expecting to receive. We often ask expecting not to receive and of course we get what we expect – nothing!

Believing we don't deserve is the greatest block to prosperity. Whatever we unconsciously believe, we will create for ourselves, so if we believe we deserve success, we are open to receiving it. If we believe we deserve prosperity, we are open to riches.

It is quite easy to test our belief in deserving. Make a list of things you want, from qualities like success to material things like a new car or house or better job. Then ask a friend to look you in the eye and tell you one at a time that you deserve these things. Notice your body responses and most important of all notice your eyes. If they slip away, then you know that unconsciously you don't believe you do deserve.

Then it is time to start affirming that you deserve.

There may be times when a wise, far-seeing father knows that if he pours riches onto a child, that child will be lazy or will not use his potential. And so he waits for an auspicious time for the child to be ready. So when it best serves the needs of our soul to be rich, then riches flow in. Sometimes poverty serves our highest purpose because it encourages us to put in effort.

I know that if I had had plenty of money when I was divorced I might never have summoned the courage to become a therapist. Because I had to earn a living I was forced to do the training, I had to find my courage, my confidence, raise my belief in myself and set up in practice.

A neighbour of mine was separating from her husband at the same time as I did. Her circumstances were very similar except that she had more money and kept the family home. I moved away and lost touch.

Seven years later she came across my name in the telephone directory and phoned me. She told me she was still living in her big house. She was lonely, bitter and blaming. Her children had left home. She didn't want to take a job. Nothing appealed to her. She didn't want to train for anything. It was too much trouble.'You're so lucky,' she said, 'to have a career.' Her voice whined and whinged and I thanked her for the call and cut the conversation short.

It was then that I really could thank the wisdom of the Universe for knowing what was best for me at that time. Being poor had served my highest need and *we get what we need not what we want*. I can now look back and say thank you for it and realize that through difficulty I found strengths, abilities and talents that I didn't suspect I possessed.

So, would you fulfil your potential if you were rich?

We often believe that if we have more there will be less for someone else. It is based on a belief in lack and not on a true understanding of Spiritual Law. Not only do we live in a limitless Universe but in one where we all create our own reality. So if one person creates more prosperity consciousness, it does not mean that there is less for someone else. It simply means he draws more prosperity from the limitless pool.

The more we open up to receive, the more we have to pass to others, so the more prosperity there is for everyone.

I find that many people who come to me as clients or come on my workshops have taken vows of poverty in other lives. These vows were impressed on the unconscious mind very deeply with rituals, ceremonies, symbols and mandalas. They were obviously appropriate for that life but not for this one. If they wish to remove the vow and it feels in accordance with their Higher Purpose I ask their unconscious mind to release the information we need to dissolve the old instruction.

Some people have a bar, or lock or symbol of poverty in their mind, which can be dissolved with light. Others may be instructed to go back into the life where they took the vow and ask for release.

So many of us unconsciously choose to live as poor people because we are afraid that what we have will be taken away or that if we spend it there will be no more. So we lock it away in the bank and all the riches we have locked away in the bank are not available to us to spend.

In the same way our qualities and gifts are not available to us if we hide them away and don't believe we can use them.

So when we want to be prosperous we must give out from our store with love, knowing it comes back to us and increases.

When we pay our bills promptly and thank the Universe for the money to pay as we write the cheque or give our credit card number, then people will pay us promptly and the Universe will fill the void in our bank account with more riches. This is the Law of Flow.

When a river is flowing properly, more water automatically takes the place of that which has flowed on. There isn't a sudden empty spot. Many people resist lack and therefore create it in their lives. The Law of Resistance says that we get what we resist. It is logical. To resist something we have to focus on it. Whatever we focus on we draw into our lives.

When Jesus said, 'Resist not evil,' he was describing the Law of Resistance and his words have been generally misunderstood.

So many of us resist poverty. We say, 'I'm fed up with being poor,' or 'I hate not having enough money,' or 'Nothing comes to me.' These are negative affirmations, as are 'I'm never lucky,' 'Our family will never be rich.' I heard a beauty the other day, 'I was born in poverty and I'll die in poverty!' We do a wonderful job of imagining poverty and thus attracting it into our lives.

So if we want prosperity we must focus on prosperity or riches or what we do want. Then we attract in what we do want instead of resisting what we don't want.

What we wish for others we get for ourselves. So it is important to bless what we do have and also bless what others have.

A farmer said to me, 'When my crops aren't doing too well I look at my neighbour's fields and if they aren't doing well, I say,'Thank goodness. It's not just me. And if they are doing better than mine I feel depressed.' I said, 'Don't do that any more. Constantly bless your neighbour's crops and you will reap benefits beyond your dreams.'

It is a mark of an old soul that they can be pleased for another's success in the midst of their own set-backs.

Bless another and you will reap the blessing. So give to others in your thoughts what you want for yourself and it will come to you. Wish another ill and you will reap the ill.

The Law of Manifestation is activated by clarity. When we are totally clear about what we want then it starts to manifest. Most of us have doubts and confusion. The first thing to do is to decide what we want and write it down. Writing anchors it in our consciousness. Then we must ask ourselves, 'Do I really want this?' bearing in mind that if we were clear we wanted it we would already have it!

So it is important to ask ourselves how having it would change our lives. What would we do with it? Would having it mean responsibilities we are not ready for? Through asking these questions we very often realize that we don't really want that big house we've always hankered after. It might mean employing staff, need constant maintenance, mean our friends would no longer want to know us, mean we would be at a further distance from friendly neigh-bours, so there would be no one to pop in. Then we can decide on the medium-sized house we really want and set that as our goal, with clarity.

Then, when we have clarity, we can write down our goal, take any steps towards it that we can and confidently expect it to manifest. We must ask for what we want to manifest in accordance with Spiritual Law.

It is no use coveting our boss's job and asking for that to manifest for us. If our boss is open to the negative vibration of our covetous thoughts he may well drop dead or become ill. In this case we bear karma because of our intervention. We too may become ill or something may happen to make us lose the job because we did not get it in accordance with Law. If we are not very evolved it may wait for the next life to happen.

What we do in this life sets up the next one.

So we ask for that job or something equivalent and we ask for it to manifest in a perfect way for the highest good of all concerned.

That way our boss may find a more congenial job and leave or he may happily take early retirement and our way to prosperity is opened up in a spiritual way.

All successful businessmen do goal setting. Very often they use the masculine energy of power and thrust and hard work to achieve their goal. This is fine. It activates the Law of Manifestation and things do manifest. However all these things can be taken away again by the Laws of the Universe, for they are quite impartial. They respond to energies. So the moment the businessman's belief in himself wavers, it can all crumble.

So much better to go into our inner silence, to listen to our inner voice, to respond to our intuition first. This means listening to our feminine energy before we set the goal and then using the masculine energy to achieve it. Then we are in tune with the Universe and we manifest what is in harmony with our lives.

Never think that the rich have it easy. There are responsibilities in being rich and as many lessons to be learnt from being wealthy as from being poor. When our material needs are taken care of we are given opportunities to focus on our inner growth and expected to use them.

FOUR

Abundance

We live in an abundant Universe and the Divine Vision for each of us is total abundance. This means total peace, harmony, love, health, prosperity and our heart's desire.

In the beginning a small child lived with his father and they had a beautiful abundant garden. Everything they could possibly want or need grew there and they tended it with love and care. As the child grew older he wanted a garden like his father. His father said, 'I'll mark a corner of the garden for you. It can be your very own garden where you can grow what you want and you can learn for yourself.' And he duly marked out a little plot for the child and one for each of the other children. Of course, the child could run and play in his father's garden whenever he wanted to and share in everything there.

The father said to the child, 'I'll make things easy for you. The soil in your plot is so rich that every single seed you sow will germinate and grow into a plant. That way you will quickly learn to grow plants that you like. As soon as you've learnt all you want to you won't need a separate plot any more. You'll work with me in the garden of abundance.'

Everything started well. The child planted in his personal plot and played in his father's garden. But gradually he became careless about pulling out weeds which grew from seeds of disharmony. Some were prickly and difficult to pull out and as he left them they grew like huge prickly cactus plants, until eventually a great cactus thicket trapped him in his garden. He couldn't get through it and so it separated him from his father's garden and that of his brothers and sisters.

Because he felt lonely and separate he felt his father and brothers and sisters didn't love him any more.

And because we believe we are separate we think the Universal Father doesn't love us any more. We are under the illusion that we have no access to Him and we stay trapped in the garden of our personal unconscious.

Little do we realize that there is a wonderland of love and abundance waiting as soon as we clear away the cacti of envy, jealousy, greed, meanness, unworthiness, anger, resentment and fear which wall off our little ego selves. Then we can enter the Divine Garden of Abundance and pick fruits of joy and happiness.

So how do we start the process of dissolving these blocks round our heart which stop us having a connection with the Divine? It is an important first step to recognize that the blocks come from us and not the other way round. The Divine energy wants to get through to us but cannot do so until we have learnt our lessons. So there is help for us every step of the way.

Our beliefs and fears are unconscious blocks to abundance. Maybe we want to open to an abundance of love. We want a relationship but somehow it never works. Here are some possible beliefs that block us from having love abundance.

> If I let people close they might find what I'm really like.
> I may be trapped
> I may get hurt
> I may be abandoned
> They might demand too much of me
> They might expect too much of me
> I'd have to share
> A relationship would take too much time
> They might only want me for my money/looks?

Similarly when we are ill or in poor health, we hold

beliefs which block us from getting better or enjoying an abundance of good health.

Possible beliefs that block us from health are.

> If I'm well no one will look after me.
> I'll have to give up my anger (anger makes us ill and can also be a motive for living)
> If I'm well people will expect me to get a better job
> If I'm well people will put expectations on me
> I'll be accountable for what I do with my life
> I'll have no excuse for not doing things or not seeing certain people.
> How else can I get love and attention

Misery is addictive. It is seductive. It is a controlling position. Possible beliefs that block us from an abundance of happiness are:

> What would I think about if I gave up misery
> What would I do with my time if I had no misery to deal with.
> While I'm sad people look after me, notice me.
> How else could I get people to do what I want?

Karma is sanskrit for comeback and every emotion we send to someone else comes boomeranging back to us. So it a Universal Law that what we wish for someone else, we wish for ourselves. If we wish another ill luck, ill luck boomerangs back to us. If we wish someone would fail an exam, that degree of failure comes to us. And if we wish someone success, we get more success. If we wish someone luck in love, more love flows through us.

So when we want abundance we must wish that everyone around us has abundance.

If you want to be a brilliant musician, wish all the musicians you know good fortune. If you want to be a recognised actor or actress, praise other actors and rejoice in their good fortune.

One of the most abundance-creating exercises we can do is this. Imagine someone you dislike or are in rivalry with receiving all that they want. Visualise it clearly and do it gladly. Then see yourself receiving all that you want too.

Your generosity creates abundance for you. And always remember that

> Forgiveness dissolves hate and revenge
> Trust dissolves suspicion
> Kindness dissolves meanness
> Generosity opens our hearts
> Unconditional love heals us and others.

We can start now to review our thoughts, our words, our motives, our lives.

Money is not abundance. We can manifest riches all alone in our cactus garden but they can be taken away. Success alone is not abundance for that too can disappear overnight.

When we know deep within us that we are a beloved child of the Universal Father, then we start to dissolve our blocks to abundance. As we link into this higher energy, we know all our needs will be met and then prosperity, love, health and peace flow through us as we become channels for the Divine.

When we know we are a beloved child then we feel lovable and worthy and act in that way.

To test your lovability and worthiness notice how you respond to compliments. Do you accept them graciously? Or do you feel suspicious as if you are sure they don't really mean it or even worse are laughing at you?

How do you receive presents? Are you grateful and pleased? Do you really wish they wouldn't bother because you have to repay? Do you feel they shouldn't go to so much trouble for you? Do you feel awkward?

We limit abundance by not allowing ourselves to receive.

Here is an important way to start changing this. The Law of Prayer is quite simple. It is, ask, believing and you will receive.

This is widely quoted and both misunderstood and ignored. It is no use saying, 'Please God, make me more generous,' and then acting in a tight fisted way. It is no use saying, 'Please God can I have a new car,' and then not expecting it to manifest. This is what most people do and it is a waste of energy.

Ask, with faith that it is granted, and it is already given to you.

It is faith that activates the Law of Prayer. Our task is to be clear about what we want, to ask for it and believe we'll get it. It is not our task to get it.

People say, 'There's no use praying for that. I can't possibly see how I can get it.' Or someone says, 'There's no use praying for a total healing. The doctors say it's incurable!' And there probably is no way that our little limited self can get it or cure it. Luckily the great Universal mind has limitless potential! God has powers that most of us don't even comprehend.So all we need to do is ask with faith. The how is up to the Universe. When we have total faith and pray for something, we are expected to act as if the prayer is already granted. That is the test of faith.

There were two women on one of my Abundance Workshops. Both wanted to move into new homes. Neither could see any possibility of finding the home she wanted nor of having the money to do so.

I explained to them they had to ask for what they wanted in the most minute detail, in other words have total clarity, and then expect it or something better to happen. I asked them to add to what they had written, 'For the Highest Good of all concerned.'

I suggested that as an act of faith they go home and pack their belongings up – as if their new home was already prepared.

Janice phoned me next day to say she had made a list of sixteen requirements for her new home. She had gone back to her apartment after the workshop and packed everything. 'I can leave here within twentyfour hours,' she told me.

I heard nothing from Madge.

Three days later Janice phoned again delirious with excitement. A friend of a friend of a friend had heard that she was looking for a new place and offered her exactly what she wanted at a rent that she could afford. She was moving in next day.

I saw Madge a month later. She had written a sort of list but it all seemed somehow impossible and she didn't really think she could get it. She told me she couldn't pack her belongings because it would have been so hurtful for the man she lived with. A year later I heard she was still in the same place – a victim of the fates and lack of faith.

Here is a story I heard Graham Browne tell on one of his very powerful Universal Training workshops. One of the men participating in a workshop had got into touch with an enormous amount of anger with his parents. He had had a terrific abreaction and released the anger and come to a totally new understanding about his parents. He went home after the workshop and was met by his little three year old daughter. He felt so good, he picked her up and gave her a huge hug, saying, 'You'll never guess what Daddy's been doing today?' The little girl looked at him gravely and said, 'You've been letting go of all the things that stopped you loving me. It was while Mummy and I were in the shops.'

She knew. She felt the change in energy. And as he dissolved his anger, he opened up to the abundance of a new relationship with his daughter.

Something very similar happened to me. I was engaged to my second husband and I was frightened of the commitment. I didn't want to get hurt. I could think of a million reasons why I would be better off on my own. As the wedding day grew nearer it seemed very scary. I knew he felt the same way. We niggled at each other and things were becoming fraught between us. We discussed it and decided we would take our houses off the market. We'd remain friends and not get married.

I took off my engagement ring and went away to think. A week later we met to discuss it again and came to the same conclusion. We had too many differences. It couldn't possibly work.

Next day I was driving along thinking about the flame of Truth. Suddenly I saw clairvoyantly a huge flame appear in front of me. As I moved towards it I saw my walls around me – rows and rows of them! No wonder the relationship couldn't work. As I moved into the Flame of Truth, the walls fell down one by one and I *knew* I could make the relationship work. It was totally up to me. All I had to do was take my walls down.

That moment of illumination probably only took a few seconds.

I drove home and put my engagement ring back on. When Eric came to see me that evening, I said. 'It's O.K. We're engaged again.'

He said, 'Yes, I know. It happened at six o'clock.'

He was in another town and he felt the change in my energy.

I took down the walls. Both houses sold immediately and our new one appeared on cue.

And because I let go of my blocks, I discovered a husband who was more generous, more kind, more loving beyond my wildest expectations. In that one instant I allowed true abundance to flow in.

FIVE

Success

Success is a belief. We can have failure consciousness or success consciousness. It takes the same amount of energy to hold beliefs of success as ones of failure. In fact it probably uses more energy to be negative because failure pictures create anxiety and anxiety uses up a lot of life force.

When we want to be successful we need to know exactly where we are going. To tell the unconscious mind that we want to be successful is like telling the bank manager we want to borrow lots of money. He is going to ask precise questions, such as 'How much?' 'What for?' etc.

We wouldn't expect to tell the travel agent that we want to go on holiday and please book it. He needs to know where we want to go, how much we want to spend. If we are still vague he will ask if we want to fly or drive, go to sun or snow, go far or near, to sea or mountains. In other words he will try to focus our minds to get clarity.

So it is much too woolly to give our unconscious mind the message that we want to be successful.

In order to succeed we decide what we want to succeed at. The more detailed the instructions, the more likely we are to attract the success we want.

It is important to be really motivated by what we want to succeed at. We need to believe in it, to enjoy it, to talk about it, to enthuse. This energises our vision. Then we have committed ourselves to success.

We can all be successful. The longest journey starts with the first step and goes on, one step at a time. The trouble is that if we set out vaguely for Edinburgh and then have a flat tyre in London, we lose heart. If we have more set backs on our route and break down half way in Manchester, we give up our goal and settle for Manchester instead.

How different if we have a burning desire to get to Edinburgh. If there is something important that we want to do or see in Edinburgh, we talk about Edinburgh. We think about it. We focus about it. We intend to get there.

Flat tyres and breakdowns are then merely hiccups on the way. Nothing short of Edinburgh will do.

Furthermore, when we are motivated and excited, when we are full of energy about our mission, we will fire other people with enthusiasm to come with us or to help us on our way.

Then it is, 'Edinburgh here we come! Success here we come!'

We can all be successful. With intention to reach our goal, with dedication, commitment and enthusiasm, we can overcome anything.

Some people have more setbacks than others. In fact the more successful we are, the more set backs we have usually coped with.

Here is a story I was once told about someone who couldn't cope with rejection. Each rejection was a major setback for him. He was a teacher and a very good one but one of the lowest paid in the school because he so feared rejection and failure he wouldn't apply for promotion.

One day, in the staffroom, he listened to the other teachers talking and they were boasting, yes, boasting, about the number of job rejections they had had.

And as he listened he realised that the more senior the teacher, the more 'failures' he had had. And the person with the most set backs of all was the Head Teacher.

So, failures and set backs aren't what they seem. They are stepping stones to success. They are strengtheners to weed out the committed from the uncommitted.

And who puts the set backs and obstacles in our Path to success. We do.

When my first book *Light Up Your Life* was due to be

published, suddenly everything went wrong. There was delay upon delay. I was in despair. Again and again I sat down to meditate on the problem. Nothing came through. I tried to look within to find how I was creating this. No answers came. One day a friend gave me the name of a soul therapist who had helped her. Her name was Lorna and I went to see her a few days later.

She took one look at me and said that I was being tested. It was totally unnecessary. The only person testing me was me (at a Higher Level). I was testing myself for strength so that I could know I could help other people when I was going through adversity. My Higher Self was testing me to show me what I was made of. Lorna assured me that everything would go ahead quickly.

It was a relief. I sat back then and waited for all to go ahead, which it did. All around me people kept telling me my aura was looking much stronger!

The Universe with its usual economy of energy killed two birds with one stone. Lorna and I became great friends. She had been told some weeks before by her guidance that someone with the same birthday as she had would be coming to her and we would do work together. She and I share a birthday and we often work together.

I serve another purpose in her life. I am much more organised than she is. When she is lazing or day dreaming at her desk, she finds me standing beside her telling her to get on with her project.

When I was in my early twenties I read a book on people who had become millionaires. The one thing I still remember from that book was this advice. 'If you wish to be a millionaire, mix with millionaires and very rich people and some of it will rub off on you.'

So if we really want to be successful, prosperous, positive and happy, then it is time to weed the miserable, negative and unsuccessful people out of our lives! It sounds harsh but we wouldn't let weeds choke our beautiful flowers. We would pull the weeds out without a second thought. So why should we let ourselves be choked by weedy people?

These weedy people are mirrors of our negative aspects and the desire to be successful tells us it is time to let go of these negative mirrors and look into positive ones. Many of us fail to become successful and reach our goals because we are confused. We let conflicting thoughts go round and round in our minds.

When we are confused we are symbolically driving round and round the Manchester ring road. Sometimes it is because we are afraid we will take the wrong road to Edinburgh. Even more likely to keep us driving round the ring road is the fact that we really are not sure where we want to go.

The solution for confusion is simple. We must go into our inner wisdom, in other words, meditate or go somewhere quiet where our mind can stop whirling and be still. Then we need to take a decision. Having taken the decision we must stick to it. If we turn back we turn to salt, like Lot's wife. We crystalize.

There is no such thing as a wrong decision. There are decisions to move or to stay stuck. In other words we either open a door and explore the possibilities or we stay in the corridor.

A decision is an energy of strength and the Universe rewards strength, so decisions activate Spiritual Law and doors open. Decisions open opportunities.

If we are taking decisions, focusing on success and know what we want, but are failing, then it is time to look at our underlying beliefs. Before we come into this life we have pre-conceptions. These are beliefs, based on our past experiences, which we hold in our subconscious, our inner computer. Our beliefs are the foundations on which we build our lives. We are each responsible for our own beliefs. The Law of Attraction says that like attracts like, so whatever we believe we attract. Thus the Universe holds in front of us a mirror of what we believe.

Imagine two people who are equally clever. We'll call them Peter and Paul. They have exactly the same intelligence. Peter believes he is stupid. Paul believes he is clever. Peter will attract people who treat him as stupid. He will attract situations which make him feel stupid. He constantly devalues his worth. Maybe he takes a lesser job than he is capable of. He creates failure.

Paul believes he is clever and attracts jobs which extend his capability. He feels confident in his ability. Because he believes he is clever, people treat him as such and he soon creates situations where he feels good and succeeds. He attracts success.

So from the same intelligence, each creates a different situation from their beliefs. It is Peter's responsibility to look at the beliefs he holds that create his failure. To find clues about the beliefs he holds, he can watch his thoughts and listen to what he says to people. Then each time he thinks failure thoughts he can stop and make positive affirmations. They are very powerful.

He can also visualize a positive outcome. This puts positive pictures into his unconscious mind. The more enthusiasm and fire he puts into this visualization the more effective it will be. The unconscious works exactly like a computer. It is programmed with pictures. Positively visualizing success will change the programming. When we set our minds on success we activate Spiritual Law and seeming miracles happen.

Jeanette was well aware of the Laws but even she was surprised at the results when she activated them. She decided she was bored with her job, that she deserved more money and a company car. She worked for a large company and decided that she wanted a double promotion to reach her goal. So she set to work to activate the Laws. She wrote down, 'I am now a manager at a salary of x pounds per year with a red company Cavalier.' She pinned the piece of paper over her bed, taped it onto the fridge, in her car, everywhere she could see the words. She drew a picture of herself sitting in a manager's office. And she made constant affirmations of success.

Then she focused her mind on being a manager. She mixed with the other managers, even sitting with them at lunch time when she could. She bought new clothes as if she had already been promoted. Within a month she had been promoted to a manager's job. She had a red Cavalier as a company car.

Her boy friend was very impressed. He was in a dead-end job and wanted to get out of it but he couldn't see a way out. He was a mechanic and had no other skills. Jeanette told him to make affirmations of new opportunities and focus on the salary he wanted. She knew that we only have to hold the goal in our vision. The Universe will find the means, and prompt us to do anything necessary. She helped him to write suitable affirmations and they awaited results. He just knew something would happen. And it did. A brand new position was created at the factory. He was asked if he would take on a job as training supervisor to train all the mechanics. He got the salary he wanted.

When we change our beliefs into positive ones we magnetise success.

SIX

The Power of Affirmations

We all have infinite potential. Within each of us lies the possibility for success, health, beauty and wonderful lives. However, when we constantly think negative thoughts, we limit or block our potential. This process can be reversed NOW.

Anything we focus on increases in our lives. We choose what we think about, talk about and reflect on. If we choose to focus on failure, we fail. If we hold success in our thoughts we must inevitably succeed. If we focus on ill health or poverty, we can create such ill health and poverty that we are crippled by it. And if we hold visions of success and wealth, or health, happiness and love, these qualities must come into our lives.

Most of us want to be joyful, strong, confident, rich and popular but don't know how to change the tapes of negative beliefs which we constantly play in our minds. One of the most effective ways to replace the old beliefs with positive wholesome ones is to make daily affirmations. An affirmation is a positive statement about ourselves or our abilities. Once impressed on our unconscious mind, the positive belief manifests in our lives.

An affirmation must pass through the critical censor before it reaches the unconscious mind. The unconscious is where we hold our belief system, so it is only when affirmations become fixed in the unconscious that we can change our beliefs, and therefore our thoughts and our lives.

It is like wanting to put a new book onto the library

shelves. In order to get into the library we must get the book past the librarian. If she doesn't recognise it as belonging in the library, she'll turn it away. So we have to slip past the librarian without attracting her attention to put the book on the shelves.

So maybe we want to put more confidence into our unconscious mind, but our censor, which is our personal librarian, doesn't recognise confidence as belonging in our belief system, so it will reject suggestions of confidence. Then we have to slip the affirmations of confidence past the censor.

Cumbersome statements alert the conscious mind, so the librarian comes out to examine the affirmation and rejects the message. This is why rhyming affirmations are so effective. The rhythm and rhyme lull the critical censor, allowing the affirmation to slip through to the unconscious mind where it can start to change our belief system and therefore the tapes we constantly run in our minds.

Resistance to Affirmations

If an appropriate rhythmic affirmation doesn't work when it has been constantly used for three weeks, there may be a deeper problem.

If we choose an affirmation for slimness, for instance, and we focus on it and flood our mind with it but we are still not becoming slim, we must check out what slimness means for us. If we then realise we would have to handle the admiration of the opposite sex, we need to choose an affirmation for increasing self worth. We use this for three weeks before returning to the slimming affirmation.

Take another example. We want to succeed at work and use an affirmation for success. Then we get the sack. Something's working! We are resisting. We must look at our beliefs about success. Do we believe we deserve success? Can we cope with success? If the former, find an affirmation about deserving. If the latter, use an affirmation about ability first. Then return to affirm success.

Resistance is showing that something within us is trying

to change or there would be nothing to resist. Our beliefs set our future and we are drawn towards this future as if towards a magnet. If we decide to change direction we are constantly pulled back towards the magnet until our affirmations change the position of the magnet. Then we can move in the new direction, magnetised towards success.

A lady attending one of my workshops became aware that she needed to become more feminine. She chose an affirmation for accepting her femininity and was pleased as she had a date the following evening. She worked hard with her affirmations and I saw her the next day before her date. She was wearing black trousers, black boots, a cravat and square cut jacket. I had never seen her looking so masculine! When I gently pointed this out to her, she laughed as she realised the extent of her resistance. She had time to go home to change into something softer and more feminine. And she was pleased to recognise that the affirmation was clearly beginning to work.

Laws of Affirmation

1. Affirmations must always be in the present tense. Life is a series of here and now moments. Our unconscious mind, which is a computer, has no concept of time, so tomorrow never comes.
2. Affirmations must only contain positive words. If we affirm that we are letting go of greed, our computer focuses on greed. So instead we must concentrate on the positivity of generosity. Even using words like forgive are better avoided as it focuses on the negativity of what we believe we have to forgive. At a higher level we are one and the person or situation has come to us to teach us a lesson we need to learn.
3. Don't use NOT. The unconscious cannot take in negatives. Check it out. Close your eyes and say, 'I don't want to see a tree'. The only picture your unconscious mind can present to you is a tree. So if you affirm that you don't want a cigarette, you are presenting your mind with a picture of a cigarette and

will crave one. Affirm instead the positive benefits of health and the joy of eating fruit.

4. The Law of Manifestation is quite simple. What we think about we create. An idea starts as thought and when we energise it with more thoughts, especially emotionally charged ones, it becomes matter. This is how we manifest the disease in our bodies and the material possessions around us. Remember we are very powerful people. Our thoughts are our health and our riches. It takes the same amount of energy to manifest riches as poverty or to be ill as healthy. So use the power of affirmation to manifest something good in your life.

5. Act as if you have already received what you affirm.

6. The Universe works with mirrors. Everyone we attract into our lives is a mirror of an aspect of us. So if we are untrustworthy or we don't trust others, we attract untrustworthy people. The moment we notice this we can start to affirm our reliability, our integrity and trust- worthiness. Then of course, when we are totally trustworthy, we can only attract trustworthy people to us. So when we change, others around us change or they leave our lives or they simply don't bother us any more.

7. We have been flooding our minds with negative messages so we must make sure we really flood our minds with the new positive ones, repeating the affirmations as many times a day as possible.

8. If we want to manifest something, rather than a quality within ourselves, we must always affirm that what we have asked for or something better will manifest for the highest good of all concerned. After all the Universe may have something much better in mind for us.

9. It adds energy to give thanks that our affirmations are already working.

10. Remember we are part of the Divine energy. God wants the best for us. The only thing that stops us having the best is our belief.

Change things today The affirmation way.

Affirmations for Self worth

Everybody values me
Because of my sincerity.

I'm balanced and in harmony
And everyone looks up to me.

I love my positivity
And the friends it brings to me.

I can now say No
If I don't want to go.

I rejoice in the birth
Of my value and worth

My every word
Is valued and heard

My strength does grow
Now I've learnt to say No.

My enthusiasm's fired
I'm valued and admired.

I'm happy to be
Accepted as me.

My confidence is high
I'm ready to fly.

I'm light, I'm bright,
I've got it right.

My mind is sharp and incisive
Clear and decisive.

Here on earth
I claim my worth.

My words are confident and clear
So people listen and they hear.

Affirmations for Success

> Today's a wonderful day
> I succeed in every way.
>
> I take the lead
> I now succeed.
>
> Success flows in
> And I win
>
> I'm slim and healthy
> Successful and wealthy.
>
> Take heed
> I can succeed.
>
> Success my aim
> My goal is fame.
>
> Business is viable
> Because I'm reliable.
>
> Money flows
> My profit grows.
>
> I set my sights
> On my name in lights.
>
> As a high flyer
> I go ever higher.
>
> I sell with zest
> For I'm the best.
>
> Light up my name
> I aim for fame.

Affirmations for prosperity

> The more I give, the more it seems
> I'm rich beyond my wildest dreams.
>
> It feels quite funny
> I'm a magnet for money.

Abundance now flows through me
As I open to prosperity.

I deserve prosperity
So great riches flow to me.

I'm a child of the Universe
And God always fills my purse.

Prosperity flows in a stream
To fulfil my every dream.

Luxuries now come my way
I enjoy them every day.

I'm as rich as can be
And it's setting me free.

Life is golden and sunny
I relax about money.

Money comes to me
And I enjoy prosperity.

Affirmations for Opportunity

New doors open up to me
A world of opportunity.

Open the door
I'm ready for more.

Affirmations for Self Love and Spirituality

Calm and centre, quiet and still
I love myself and always will.

I'll go to any length
To walk my path with strength.

Like a rock I'm steady.
I am strong and I am ready.

All day long
I'm centred and strong.

I am quiet and calm and still
Listening to the Higher Will.

All is dissolved
My problems solved.

As I hear my inner voice
Each decision's a wise choice.

I shut out the worldly din
And hear the still wise voice within.

I connect now to my Source
And answers come of course.

To find deep repose
I relax my toes (do it)
The energy flows
Up to my nose (let it)
Where I focus on breathing
Till the thoughts stop seething
I'm quiet and still
Then I hear God's will.

Affirmations for safety

Protected by my inner glow
I am safe wherever I go.

I grow stronger and stronger every day
Safe and secure in every way.

I'm guarded and guided
My needs all provided.

My inner light strong and steady
I am safe and I am ready.

I'm safe and secure
Guided and sure.

I totally know
It's safe to let go.

I feel very strong
For I know I belong.

Affirmations for tests and exams

Work sinks deep into my mind
Exams are easy now I find.

I do my best
And pass the test.

Sharp and clear
My mind's in gear.

I'm ready and primed
It's all in my mind.

My mind is keyed.
It's time to succeed.

Affirmations for happiness

A hug a day
Is the happiness way.

Life is joyous. Life is fun.
Happiness has now begun.

I proclaim
Joy's my aim.

I've won
Life's fun.

I cheer and shout hooray
Today is a wonderful day

I start each day
In a bright happy way.

I'm happy and bright
A channel for light.

I fill up my day
The happiness way.

Affirmations for letting go of the past

> You are you and I am me
> I let you go and I am free.
>
> Past is past and done is done,
> My new life has now begun.
> Every single day is bright
> I'm now creating love and light.

Affirmations for charm and beauty

> My beauty's alluring
> For joy is enduring.
>
> I walk with grace
> And a smiling face.
>
> Let happiness show
> I shimmer and glow.
>
> I am a shining star
> Seen by all near and far.
>
> When I smile I glow
> With beauty I know.
>
> With a friendly smile I greet
> All the people that I meet.
>
> I speak on the phone
> In a warm and friendly tone.

Affirmations for Life Force

> I'm full of life and fire
> My energy is growing higher.
>
> I feel so good today
> A miracle's sure to come my way.
>
> I gather all my strength and might
> To stick with what I know is right.

I see the best in everyone
And their responses make life fun.

Today is a miracle day
I'm enjoying it in every way.

I go to any length
To find my inner strength

Affirmations for healing the inner child

The past we now release
As I fill my child with peace.

I skip and dance and jump and play
With my child every day.

I am feeling warm and mild
Cradling my inner child.

I look younger every day
As I allow my child to play.

I have found it very effective to give people very simple affirmations to use as if they are the stuck child. For instance, a lady who never felt accepted as a child imagined herself as seven years old as she made this affirmation and found it helped her enormously.

I'm happy and free
And accepted as me.

Similarly, a man who was never chosen or wanted at school imagined himself back in childhood with this affirmation to free his inner child.

Now I'm the chosen one
Everything in life is fun.

In order to be creative and joyful we must give our inner child permission to play.

I run and skip and sing and play
And enjoy myself in every way.

Affirmations for relaxation and play

I now let myself play
At least once every day.

I now let go
And trust the flow.

I'm now slowing down the pace
To find myself some time and space.

As I relax and play each day
I hear what my inner voice does say.

Every thought is warm and kind,
As I now relax my mind.

My world is safe, my world is kind,
That's the picture in my mind.

Relaxed and safe I soothe my mind,
Letting go I now unwind.

Yes I must
Relax and trust.

Let it go
Take it slow
And feel the flow.

Healing Relationships

Past is past and done is done
Dad (Mum) and I are truly one.

I explain just how I feel
So our relationship can heal.

My heart opens like a flower
With love I reclaim my power.

As I understand your past

Old wounds heal at last.

My relationship is good
I'm loved and understood.

I affirm that I now can
Attract the perfect man.

It's safe to be real
And express how I feel.

Affirmations for Sexuality

Being gay

I chose to be gay
This time round
And great learnings
I have found.

This is my way
I choose to be gay.

It's O.K. by me
I'm gay and I'm free.

I'm proud to be gay.
I'm proud to be me.
I'm proud of my sexuality.

Accepting sexuality

Uninhibited and free
I enjoy my sexuality.

I know it's safe for me
To claim my sexuality.

I'm a woman and I rejoice
That I made this excellent choice.

I'm a man and I think it's great
That I chose manhood for my fate.

I know now what I didn't know then

I'm really attractive to men.

It's good to know
I can say No.

Accepting womanhood
Makes me feel good.

I act with poise
When I'm with boys.

Affirmations for healing the body

We all hear and see selectively. As we choose to see and
hear differently, our physical body changes.

My eyes are open and I see
Only beauty all round me.

My eyes are open and I see
Everyone is loving me.

As I listen I can hear
Which direction I must steer.

I'm willing to hear
So all is made clear.

I choose to hear
What soothes my ear.

Walking down a leafy country lane in the middle of
nowhere,two women appeared behind me, talking in shrill
voices. I wondered how I had attracted this disharmony.
Was I being shown I wasn't in harmony myself? Yet I felt
still and centred. As I walked I suddenly heard.

I transform the sounds I hear
Into music for my ear.

Those shrill women were a lesson in remaining in
harmony whatever the circumstances. I turned their voices

into a tinkling stream and they soon turned off onto
another path.

This affirmation can help enormously if we have noisy
neighbours or are disturbed by barking dogs or traffic
sounds. It is our perception of the sound which annoys us.
When our mind hears the noise differently it need no
longer disturb us. If we have problems making changes in
our lives, this may reflect in our joints. If we are inflexible
about something, our joints become inflexible. And of
course, they bend, and just like the bend in a river, this is
where silt forms if we have disharmony flowing through
us. So negativity silts up our joints and needs to be flushed
free with love. Pleasing others and burying our resentment
is one of the commonest causes for dis-ease.

> I release what angers me
> In doing so I heal my knee.

> I oil my joints with thoughts of love
> And trust all change to heaven above.

> Every loving thought now frees
> Wrists and elbows, ankles, knees.
> I'm ready to understand
> In doing so I heal my hand.

> Everyone knows
> I love my nose.

> Now nothing taxes
> My back relaxes.

> My back is straight
> I just can't wait
> To show I'm strong
> All life long.

> As I daily am more wise
> I regularly exercise.

> My body now responds to me
> With health and vitality.

> My load is gone
> My shoulders strong.

I watch my thoughts
And set love free
And this love
Is healing me

My heart now mends
As I let in new friends.

I now belong
And my heart feels strong.

My throat is open
My voice is clear
I speak the Truth
For all to hear.

My nails grow long
And very strong.

What a treat
To enjoy happy feet.

I am a perfect size
I have beautiful thighs.

My beauty within
Reflects in my skin.

SEVEN

Changing Unconscious Learnings

When we have experienced something a number of times our unconscious mind takes this in as a learning. It then becomes a truth as far as we are concerned and limits our lives unless we can change it.

I was once told this story as an illustration of how easy it is to become conditioned, and totally believe that conditioning.

There was a big fish tank in which minnows and a pike swam. Naturally the pike used to eat the minnows. However, one day a glass screen was put in between the pike and the minnows. Over time the pike learned that every time it went to eat a minnow, it hit the glass and got a sore nose. So the pike believed a minnow meant only a sore nose. When the glass screen was removed, the pike starved in a tank full of minnows.

We can be lonely in a world full of love if we believe we are unlovable And just as the pike thought it was protecting itself by leaving the minnows alone, so our unconscious mind takes in information and tries to protect us. Most of the time it does an amazingly good job of discriminating between the appropriate and inappropriate.

Unlike that pike, we make constant new helpful learnings. However, it may take a few weeks or months to change a learning. A friend of mine, Robert, told me how he was driving through a nearby town. When he turned right, his car was involved in an accident. His head was cut open and he was taken to hospital for stitches.

Pretty soon he was back behind the wheel and the next

time he signalled to turn right he was surprised to find he
had a stabbing pain at the point of his head injury. The
stabbing pain stopped as soon as he had accomplished the
turn.

His unconscious mind was, of course, reminding him
that it was dangerous to turn right. These 'reminders'
continued for six months. By then his unconscious mind
had re-learned that it was safe to turn right and the
stabbing pains stopped. Sometimes, however, our unconscious mind holds onto warning signals in a seemingly
unhelpful way. A girl of fifteen called Rosemary was
brought to me by her mother because she fainted when she
passed tall buildings. Her auntie lived in a tall block of flats
and the girl couldn't even visit her. Fainting or becoming
unconscious is of course the ultimate in self protection.

Rosemary came from a stable family. She was pleasant,
outgoing and there appeared to be no other phobias or
difficulties. Her mother couldn't think of anything that had
happened during the child's life which could account for
the fainting.

Rosemary went deeply into hypnosis on her first visit
and her unconscious mind revealed that when she was ten
months old she was learning to stand. She was with her
father and grandfather and standing between them. They
weren't looking after her, and she had slipped and fallen on
the kerb into the road. Because she was so tiny, this was
terrifying. Everything seemed huge and her unconscious
mind had retained an imprint that tall buildings were
dangerous. By causing her to faint, her unconscious mind
believed it was protecting her from terrible danger each
time she passed one of these tall buildings.

I hoped that now the source of her problem had been
brought to conscious awareness, Rosemary's unconscious
mind would let go of the necessity to protect her. But it
said, no. She must have her confidence built up. I worked
with her for two sessions, building confidence into her
unconscious mind in hypnosis and re-programming it
with appropriate information. Then she found she could
easily pass tall buildings and visit her aunt.

Many people have full blown panic attacks or mild panicky feelings for no seeming reason. They can't understand why. It is always worth looking for the source of the problem. Panic feelings, the heart thumping, palms sweating, flushing, wanting to go to the loo, diarrhoea, are all ways of the body preparing itself to flee from danger.

I once had a relationship with a man I thought I was going to marry. We had a few days holiday together and everything seemed fine. I said goodbye to him on the Sunday evening and looked forward to his next phone call. On the Tuesday, he telephoned me and said the relationship was over. It was a profound shock.

Years passed. I had no relationships that engaged my heart until I met my second husband, Eric. When we first met I used to see him at weekends and he used to phone me during the week. As our relationship became closer I found my heart was racing and I felt slightly sick and sweaty whenever the phone rang on Monday or Tuesday. I couldn't understand why I was having these panic feelings.

It wasn't until I sat quietly to tune in to what was going on for me that I realized what was happening. As a result of my previous experience, my unconscious mind had taken on board the belief that, when you love someone, he may phone and finish the relationship suddenly. This was clearly dangerous, so my unconscious primed me to flee from the danger. As soon as Eric phoned during the week, my unconscious recorded that the danger was over and the panics stopped.

The moment I brought the reason for the panics to conscious awareness, they stopped. Very often just understanding our process helps to heal us. If we suppress our feelings at the time of a problem, then the imprint of the suppressed emotion is held in the cells of our body. The memory lies dormant until it is triggered. This may be lifetimes later!

We saw with Robert that the memory was triggered as soon as he left hospital and started to turn right in his car.

With Beth, the imprint of deeply suppressed emotion lay dormant for much longer.

She was living with her fiancé, John but was terrified of committing herself to marrying him. She made many awarenesses during her first two sessions and I was really surprised when she didn't turn up for her third session.

Next day she telephoned to say that she had been violently ill in bed with a stomach bug and hadn't been able to get out of bed for four days. I asked her to think what might have caused such a violent stomach upset. She said she would give it some thought. She bounded in for her next appointment saying, 'I know what the sickness was. I had a bit of a row with John and he said he didn't trust me. I immediately felt sick and started being sick that night.' She added that she was very rarely sick. It seemed as if the words, 'I don't trust you,' were a trigger.

Using the trigger words, 'I don't trust you,' I asked her to feel how that felt in her body and then go back to her first memory of that feeling. She recalled her first experience of this not-being-trusted feeling in this life when her mother had blamed her for something she hadn't done. We worked to satisfy the hurt feelings she had had as that child and then I took her back to the first time she recorded that same feeling in her memory banks.

She went straight back to the ninth century when she had betrayed her husband, the same man who was now her fiance, and her cells were still imprinted with a memory of the dire consequences. So, many lifetime's later, when her fiancé said, 'I don't trust you,' the cells of her stomach remembered and reacted in a violent physical way.

Small wonder Beth had found it so difficult to commit to marriage. At an unconscious level, she was constantly replaying the memory of how dangerous marriage to this man had been. By bringing the old memories to consciousness and working on them, she was able to release the fear and finally she did get married.

For many people it is an essential part of the healing to

work through the suppressed emotions. And at other times just seeing other lives without any emotional input or involvement helps people to take decisions which can change their current lives.

Paulette had long curly hair and enormous brown eyes. She was very angry with her husband and felt quite justified in having a lover.

It was quite an unexpected and intriguing experience for her to find herself in a past life where her husband kept her under constant guard. She spent the whole of that life feeling angry with this possessive husband and kept trying to escape. She took one of the guards as her lover just to spite her husband.

She lived that life with her heart closed towards him. So I asked her to imagine herself back in that life with her heart open. She saw at once that her husband had only imprisoned her because she didn't love him and he was frightened of losing her. As soon as she opened her heart to him, she saw that he trusted her and was confident to let her be free.

She was very shocked by what she had experienced. When she went home she was much warmer and more open with her husband. Her husband became so much nicer that she started to feel guilty about having a lover.

When she came back for another session, she wanted to have a clearer picture of her past life links with her husband and lovers. She flipped from lifetime to lifetime. She observed that in each one she had protected herself by having a lover. This divided her energy and meant she never committed properly to her husband of that life.

Within a few days she finished her relationship with her lover. After seeing it all so clearly, she wasn't going to repeat the pattern yet again. She committed herself to her husband and phoned me frequently to tell me how wonderful and kind and thoughtful her husband was. She couldn't believe she had ever hated him.

One of the positive benefits of working with past lives is that it disengages the ego. Because it feels less personal when the story happens once removed, we can see our shadow aspects at work, without having to defend ourselves. I think it would have taken Paulette a lot of work on this life to achieve a similar result with her husband, because she was very attached to her belief that all the problems were caused by him and that she was powerless in the situation.

Peter felt similarly powerless. However, his feelings were much more deeply entrenched. He had felt totally powerless all this life. He had been long term depressed. He couldn't visualise or picture anything or anyone. He couldn't even remember feelings.

I don't know why I agreed to see him again. Before his second visit, I sat thinking, 'I'm sure I can't help him. What on earth can I do?' Almost immediately my Guidance said, 'You can't do anything. Step aside. You're a channel. Let us take over.'

Of course!

When he arrived I had no idea what to do to help him, so I asked him to relax and focus on the feeling of breathlessness he had been describing.

At once he found himself, in another life, inside a pyramid. He had been an important priest with many powers. He described vividly what was happening as he betrayed the people he was supposed to be serving. He died alone in shame and poverty.

In front of him he saw all the people he had betrayed. Many of them he recognised from this life as people who were causing him problems. In this life he felt totally powerless against them. He recognised that his healing lay in obtaining forgiveness from the souls he had betrayed and even more importantly in forgiving himself. It was relatively easy for him to feel them forgiving him.

He told me that he could forgive himself but I had no sense of forgiveness taking place in his heart. (It is often so difficult to forgive ourselves). Perhaps at some level he wanted to go through with the karma.

When we talked about the session afterwards, he said he

felt the awarenesses he had had were tremendously important and helped him to understand certain people and
situations in his current life.

I don't know how much he let the awarenesses help him
for he phoned to say he felt a lot better and couldn't afford
to come for another session.

I always felt he came to give me an important lesson in
letting go of my ego and trusting the Higher Power to do
the necessary work!

When we raise our vibrations, then let go and trust, the
Higher Powers can work miracles through us.

EIGHT

Choosing Our Careers

One day the phone rang and I was asked if I would give a talk about the reasons why people chose their careers or jobs. The lady who phoned said it was very obvious why some people chose their work but why did others run businesses they could never have imagined themselves in, or do work which didn't seem right for them.

The talk was months away and I put the question into the back of my mind. Gradually, threads began to emerge – I saw coloured ribbons – and was shown that we bring in various threads and weave them into our lives.

Imagine that someone has been weaving certain colours into a tapestry. At the end of the day she puts it down and goes to bed. Next time she picks it up, she continues with those colours. She may have finished with one particular colour, of course, and she may decide to introduce some new colours, but mostly she will continue the former colour theme.

Naturally we choose which coloured threads to work on in each lifetime for the growth of our soul and our choice of career will depend on the particular shades we are weaving in. If we do not have a chance to draw certain threads into our work, then we will have to express them in our leisure time.

If we bring in violet we will choose artistic creative work or have to express this in some way in our life.

With a deep blue thread running through our lives, we will be drawn to healing or counselling or helping others with mental problems.

A turquoise thread means that we will want to communicate. We couldn't be a radio broadcaster, for instance, without this colour to weave into our tapestry. We may be drawn to lecturing or teaching or conciliating in some way.

A green thread means that we want to be involved with nature, with gardening, trees or plants for instance. We may express it in working with small children or animals, with simplicity, for it is the colour of the heart centre.

If yellow is the predominant colour in our life picture, we will have a logical, thinking, intellectual mind. To be an accountant for instance, we would have to have plenty of yellow threads. We would need this to be a bank worker, clerk, computer programmer, actuary or financier.

A person working an orange thread into their career would not be content to work alone, for it is a gregarious, people orientated colour. It could be expressed in cooking or possibly in sexuality.

With red we would need to have a job where we could use physical energy. We couldn't cope with a job that kept us chained to a desk all day.

For many of us our job or career is pre-chosen. For instance, Mozart had evidently had lifetimes as a musician and brought the musical thread predominantly into this life. His work was pre-destined but his lessons were to develop other threads to keep him grounded.

Many wonderful creative people bring in great talent, which flows automatically into their choice of work. These people sometimes struggle to deal with material life and with relationships. The threads they are working on may be beautiful ethereal colours – pale mauves and violets and peach for instance. However a beautiful tree painted in a picture in beautiful ethereal colours would look out of place without the balancing green of the leaves and brown of the branches.

So if we are well grounded we can make our business in beauty financially viable, whether it is restoring antiques or painting or being a florist or creating beautiful clothes.

Most of us are driven by karma. We bring both our talents and our karmic responsibilities into choosing work.

For example, if we have been a cruel heartless tax collector or money lender in a past life, we may decide to repay by helping people with their accounts.

A good solicitor will have a yellow intellectual thread and will also have been interested in justice and balance in other lives. If he has developed a blue thread he could become a barrister, allowing him to speak out successfully in court. To be a wise judge, a golden thread of wisdom, would need to have been earned.

So the more threads of colour we have developed in our past lives, or even in this one, the more gifts and talents we have and the more opportunities are open to us.

Many souls come in for service. We may be driven to serve others in order to expatiate for our past misdeeds. We can do this by teaching, healing, counselling or equally by working as a plumber or carpenter. It is not what we do but how we do it that counts as service.

Others of us may have volunteered our life in service to mankind to heal, teach or quietly raise people's consciousness. This is then an offering of our soul, without karma involved.

We are drawn to work where we can face our fears.

Benny was an insurance salesman. He believed totally that he was saving people from the terrible effects of disaster. He told me he became deeply upset when people didn't realize they must protect their families. Benny had been attracted to that work so that he could constantly face his own fear of disaster.

Doctors are dealing with their own fears of illness and mortality. Some doctors keep patients and their relatives in ignorance of the fact that they are seriously ill or dying. They can't face other people's emotions because they can't deal with their own. They have placed themselves in the perfect position to learn. To heal others, they need a blue thread.

With lighter healing blue and lots of green heart colour we may want to become nurses and devote ourselves to healing, caring and nurturing others.

Psychiatrists are often drawn to look at their beliefs

about sanity and the understanding of the mind. They will be following indigo threads. So too will psychotherapists, who are drawn to this work as a way of healing themselves and promoting their own inner growth. When we work with a client, we work with ourselves too at some level. So hypnotherapists too are speeding their inner growth. Some are dealing with issues of power and learning to use it with wisdom.

Spiritually inclined therapists, medics, healers, who become spiritual teachers must have a thread of gold so they can impart wisdom from other lives. In order to lecture and share this wisdom, they would need turquoise. Physical therapists who touch the body are drawn to their vocations by the need to touch. This can be a projection of their desire to be touched and nurtured on a physical level. Mostly they will have a thread of healing blue which they feel drawn to use.

At the lower end of the scale they could be bringing in murky red or orange threads, where they are drawn to touching bodies to satisfy other sexual needs within themselves. This can apply to any job or career where there is an element of touch or voyeurism.

Many of us are choosing to be born now to use healing knowledge that we have learned in previous lives. We are drawn to natural therapies ranging from herbalism, reflexology or shiatsu to astrology or crystal healing.

Red is the colour of energy and drive and get up and go. If we are drawn to a dangerous job where our lives depend on quick reactions, we will be activating a red thread.

A dynamic, grounded business person would need a bit of red in his life to succeed. If we need to express a lot of physical energy, for instance, we may be attracted to boxing. If we are very aggressive the red thread could be quite lurid. If the red thread is dark or dingy, we may be cruel within our work. The clearer and brighter the red, the greater the integrity we bring to our red work, whether as a soldier, a butcher, a sportsperson or policeman.

A dancer wants to express creatively through the body. If we like to dance to a heavy beat music we use red energy. If we are a light ethereal ballet dancer, expressing pure spirit, our thread could become light pink.

Someone who has been a sailor in other lives may love the element of water. If he can't work with water, he may unconsciously seek a career where he can be near water – with a blue streak he could be a sailing instructor for instance, with red he may build swimming pools, or with violet he may create water gardens.

Cooks use their energy to nourish others. This may be pure, loving service – an orange thread. Many, however, need emotional nourishment themselves and so they project their need out and offer to others what they most need themselves.

If someone was a baker in another life and also chose to be born into a family of cooks, he has a karmic and genetic pull which will doubly draw him to becoming a baker again. Maybe he will want to be more creative this time, or more independent and build his business acumen.

In each life we try to extend ourselves, brightening our colours and bringing in new ones.

If we are working mainly with green threads then we will be immersed in nature. Our natural pull will be towards gardening or forestry or being a nurseryman. If we can't do this we will try to work as close to nature as possible, perhaps with animals or small children or simply outdoors. Maybe we'll have to settle for having gardening or walking as a hobby.

So with different threads to put into our careers and jobs why would we choose a job which is boring, dull, repetitive or safe? If we choose a job simply because it is safe then we are working through the grey of our limiting beliefs.

We may, for karmic reasons, be imprisoned in a defective body only able to do simple work while our heart and mind may be soaring to great heights. We may be an unevolved soul who simply can't cope with anything more difficult or we may be an evolved soul testing itself in patience and endurance.

If we have been very creative, artistic and right-brain

orientated in several lives, developing our blue, violet and purple spectrum, we may decide to balance ourselves in this life by doing left brain work like accounts, thinking, logical, intellectual work. It is not always easy for us to draw in new colours. Someone struggling to bring in yellow after lifetimes of blues may appear not to be doing very well in worldly terms. In terms of growth he may be doing better than someone who is successful! There can be no judgement of another's pathway.

When we are inclined to be over imaginative or emotional, intellectual work is very grounding. If we have our own business, there is nothing like dealing with the nitty-gritty of paperwork to bring us back to earth.

Conversely, if we are very left brain orientated and have had a series of thinking yellow lives where we have been much in our heads, then we may need to develop our creative right brain and may try to paint or write imaginative stories. Or we may need to get in touch with our emotions or feelings more. If we have a legal thread we may evolve from a financial lawyer to a divorce one, or if we are on a teaching ray, we may move from teaching physics to teaching drama.

Really successful business people are psychic and intuitive. It is possible of course to be successful by using thriving, thrusting masculine power only, but the business won't last. Those empires eventually crumble. But if we use masculine and feminine energy in balance, if we listen to our intuition and back it up with energy and drive, then success is assured.

Many of us are now choosing to live a life in two or three parts so we can experience much and develop the colours of our tapestry as much as possible. Women commonly in our culture are starting with one type of work, then taking on the responsibility of a family, then re-training for a different career. Even men nowadays are changing career midstream and developing themselves as whole people.

Debbie, who was the original illustration in chapter one of the leopard who can change her spots, started developing her red thread. She was punitive and authoritarian and was drawn to being a policewoman. Then, still in her left brain, thinking mode she became an accountant and worked on her yellow parts. Gradually she moved to working with people where she had to communicate a great deal, thus developing her blue colouring and she is now a spiritual teacher and psychic, developing her indigo, purple and violet colours. All this in one lifetime!

NINE

Attracting Our Lessons

Everything and everybody that comes into our orbit is there to teach us something.

As with all matters spiritual, if we genuinely want to know what we are to learn and we ask for an answer, it will be given. Our task is to remain alert for these answers. They may come in a sudden thought or certain words people say. The answer may even be in a book or a tape or something we hear on radio or television. They may be drawn to our attention by something in our physical world.

Mark's flat was burgled three times. He couldn't work out why he had attracted these burglaries. He commented to me that it had enabled him to replace some of his old possessions with new, as he had a new for old insurance policy.

As we talked he realized that the burglaries were symbolically showing him that it was time to clear out certain old emotional patterns and replace them with new ones. He knew exactly what he had to do.

A wise lady said to me once. 'Our house is protected like a fortress and still burglars get in. They only ever take things from my husband's collection. He is hoarding those things and no one ever sees them. He gets so angry when burglars come in and take them and doesn't realise that he isn't meant to hold on to them and it is time for them to go.'

The Universe was drawing to his attention lessons in letting go. *Nothing can leave us unless it is time for it to go.*

Our attention may be drawn to our health or an emotional or physical block by something symbolic.

So if our car battery goes flat, we can perhaps ask in what area of our lives we need re-charging, emotional, mental, physical or spiritual.

Water is usually to do with emotions, so if the washing machine floods, pipes leak, the washer goes in the tap, the car radiator leaks, there is something emotional to look at.

One Christmas I was having the entire family for lunch. It was expected of me and I was always willing. Underneath I didn't want to cook for everyone. I had worked very hard all year and I wanted to be nurtured. But my powerfully ingrained patterns of being a good mother, good daughter and nurturer wouldn't let me say so.

The Universe has a way of showing us where we are not taking responsibility for our feelings. As always everything was beautifully organised. The lunch table was laid the night before and looked magnificent with crackers and decorations and shimmering cut glass. In the early hours of the following morning the pipe in the bathroom leaked. It leaked right onto the middle of the dining room table!

I was not in any doubt what the Universe was trying to tell me.

Cars are a reflection of us too. We get a slow puncture and can start asking ourselves who or what is slowly deflating us or taking our energy. The tyre goes flat. Are we exhausted? Is our life emotionally flat? We have a near miss. Are we cutting corners at work perhaps? The clutch snaps. Has our anger already snapped or is it about to? The radiator boils dry. Perhaps we need to find an appropriate way to let off steam instead of seething?

A friend was supporting herself in an unfulfilling office job while she was trying to launch into a new business. She had borrowed money to help launch her new enterprise.

I phoned her just before her advertising campaign started. She told me that the back suspension on her car had gone on her way to work. She had had to drive over a cobbled courtyard. As she got out of the car her back went at the base of her spine. This is our vulnerable area when we feel emotionally and financially unsupported.

She decided the broken suspension was telling her she

wasn't cushioning herself against the hurts of the past. I wondered if it was telling her she didn't feel cushioned against the insecurity of the future.

Our animals are a reflection of us, both our physical selves and our emotional beings. A client said to me that he was normally a good judge of people but he couldn't make his boss out. He didn't trust him but he didn't understand why.

I asked him if his boss had any animals and if so what they were like. 'Yes he's got a bull terrier. It seems very docile but he warned me not to go too near it as it can bite. Apparently he has had two other dogs which have had to be put down for attacking people.'

I suggested that my client be wary of his boss. Animals show parts of our character that we try to cover up. It could well be that his boss had a savage attacking streak. The client heeded my words and was glad he did. When his boss turned nasty, he had his back covered.

Hilary Graham is a wonderful therapist and old friend. I was staying with her on one occasion and she was complaining that her legs ached and it was really uncomfortable but she couldn't pin-point the cause. We chatted for some time about various matters and then her little cat came in. Hilary laughed. 'Oh, here comes Chloe,' she said. 'Walking all stiff legged like she does when she feels rejected.' It was my turn to laugh. 'I think you've just had your answer about your aching legs.'

Incidentally, animals reincarnate just as people do. They are on their own Spiritual Path. When we love an animal we don't lose them when they die. They come back to be with us in other lives. Chloe had been in other lives with Hilary. They were old friends.

If we have two animals, each with a different temperament, they are showing us opposite sides of our own nature. I know someone with two dogs. One is outgoing and independent. The other is timid and frightened. This woman is always in control of life, very busy and seemingly independent.

She likes the independent dog. The other one annoys

her. We always dislike mirrors of our repressed parts. Probably she has never had permission to acknowledge the timid, frightened side of her personality, so the dog acts it out for her.

If we keep missing the bus, what aren't we getting on with in our lives? Are we letting opportunities slip by? If three things happen to us together, we can be absolutely certain that our guide or teacher is trying to draw our attention to something.

So, if our telephone goes dead, our answerphone packs up and the front door bell refuses to work, who aren't we communicating with or what aren't we listening to? Alternatively, do we need to cut ourselves off and have a rest or perhaps get on with something different?

We singe something we are ironing, a spark marks the hearthrug and we burn the pan, what are we burning angry about in our lives?

We may see three lame animals or people one day. What are we being lame about? Where in our lives aren't we moving forward?

Here is an example of someone who brought together three different things that happened to her. She thought it was a nasty co-incidence that they all came at the same time!

Babs was very much into suppression and denial. It was her coping mechanism because she found it so painful to look at her childhood. She arrived for one session saying she had had a really bad week. Her car had broken down, her bathroom had flooded and she had hurt her hip. She didn't think these things meant anything or that they were connected – just bad luck.

She told me that the car broke down as she was going to an evening class. She didn't really enjoy going because it was too much effort. We gently probed her feelings at that time and she could see with a flash of clarity that the car broke down as a reflection of her feeling that it was too much effort to go on in life

We looked at the flooded bathroom. 'What happened just before you found the bathroom flooded?' I asked.

'I phoned a friend and she had visitors. She said she'd phone back and that felt absolutely fine.

'Then I went upstairs and found the ballcock in the loo had come off. The water had overflowed flooding the bathroom.

We examined the symbolism of the ballcock detaching, allowing the water to overflow. She realized that when she became detached from her feelings the water (emotions) overflowed, but she suppressed them.

With this awareness Babs was prepared to re-examine her feelings about her friend being too busy to speak to her. It transpired there was quite a background of rejected feelings. She admitted that she had thought her friend didn't want her as a friend any more.

As she made the connection with the rejection the tears flowed. Pain is cumulative and up came the suppressed pain she felt as a child when her mother didn't want her. This was pain she held deep in her heart.

When we suppress pain, whether emotional or physical, we keep it alive inside us. Her acknowledgement and flow of tears started a healing process.

Finally Babs looked at what was happening when she hurt her hip. 'I was very angry because my car broke down. I had to wait for a bus. I felt very *lonely*. I thought, *"There's no one to look after me."*'

I asked her to find the lonely space inside her and all her middle felt achingly empty. When she explored the emptiness she found herself as a little child sitting in there, quite alone.

So the Universe created her car to break down, detached the ballcock in her loo and caused her to hurt her hip, all within a short space of time so that she was forced to take notice and acknowledge where she had to work on herself.

Babs was quite awestruck that three incidents in one week could be so revealing to her.

When Babs found the little lonely child inside herself, I asked her to bring in her inner parent to take care of the child. Babs watched her inner mother walk in, go up to the child and push it away. Babs gasped in horror as the significance of this struck her. Her mother had always pushed her away, so consequently that was what Babs unconsciously did to herself. She now became very aware of this. She brought a loving caring parent into her inner scene who looked after the child and helped her to feel loved. She agreed to bring this loving caring mother in every day to talk to her little child.

What is done to us as children we continue to do to others and ourselves until we take responsibility for parenting ourselves in a different way.

Whatever happens to me I know it is the Universal Wisdom trying to teach me something. And if something happens to me three times I know that the Universe is really trying to draw my attention to something.

If three clients present with similar problems, I recognise that I need to look for the problem within myself.

There was a time when I had several bulimic clients who were bingeing and making themselves sick. I knew I had no tendency in that direction so that the lesson must be metaphorical.

As food is symbolic of love or emotional nourishment, I looked at how I was handling this in my life at that time. I quickly recognised that I was falling into an old defence mechanism. I opened up and drew certain friends towards me and received lots of emotional nourishment. Then when they became too close, it felt dangerous and I would become busy and push them out again.

As soon as I made the connection, I was able to talk to the people I did pull-push with and change the situation.

We can't heal others beyond the point we have healed ourselves any more than we expect to teach advanced Latin when we only understand elementary.

When we heal ourselves, we automatically heal others around us for they pick up our healed energy.

I was not surprised when my bulimic clients all made a sudden shift in their therapy.

No one is healed in isolation. Each healing or awareness we make within ourselves spreads to everyone in our orbit. So when we change ourselves, we add to Light in the Universe.

Healing something deep within us and letting it spread is similar to spreading a smile. When we wake up feeling good, we smile at the postman, the newsagent, the ticket collector, who are all touched by our smile and spread it. Then we continue to spread the smile all day and the ripples flow on and on, touching more and more people.

Smiles are catching. So is consciousness.

TEN

Resolving Inner Conflict

People often say they don't know who they are because they have a whole lot of conflict going on inside them. And it does sometimes feel as if there is a whole room of personalities inside us, each trying to get its voice heard and telling us something different. Each voice has its own demands and opinions and we are often very confused.

Sometimes there is such a conflict of personalities within us that it is as if there is a civil war going on. It can be exhausting.

In any classroom of children you are going to find a variety of personalities. If one child is disruptive or cheats or bullies, it doesn't mean that the whole class is bad. It just means that individual children need help. They need to be heard.

Don't forget it is often the disruptive personalities in the classroom which make the loudest noise or cause most trouble. And because it causes a problem in our psyche, we are inclined to shut out the dissenting inner voice, and refuse to listen to what it is trying to say. In just the same way, if there is a bullying child in a class, the teacher tends to squash him or punish him. The teacher usually feels angry and speaks to him accordingly.

The little bully is trying to say, 'I feel powerless. I feel unloved and I don't know how to get love and attention except by hurting others. Help me! Help me!'

When the class teacher punishes him, it verifies the little bully's belief that he's bad and unloved, so he becomes worse or buries the bullying behaviour and does something else, such as internalising it into depression.

The wise teacher finds time for the child, listens to him, encourages his talents and helps him to make friends. This is what we need to do with our dissident inner personalities.

Depending on how we perceive that our parents dealt with us as children, we develop a teacher to take charge of our classroom of inner personalities. This teacher tries to take decisions and do his best for the class as a whole. However, he may be weak or confused, in which case our inner personalities will probably run riot and we will almost certainly find decision taking difficult.

He may be cruel or sadistic or critical. In this case our inner personalities will feel cowed or put down or intensely rebellious. Some of us may have an inner teacher who is very intellectual and doesn't know how to acknowledge our emotional needs. Others may have in charge a very emotional teacher who doesn't bother to think things through and probably lands us in a mess.

When our inner teacher becomes fair and wise and nurturing and encouraging, we can integrate our sub-personalities, pacify and understand the dissident voices and encourage the bored or disillusioned ones – and allow our gifted parts to grow and develop.

Pam had for many years been a housewife and mother and now that her children were growing up she had started to set up a business at home. Her work involved helping and healing people. She was extremely gifted and was passionately involved with this work. She felt it was an important contribution to the spread of Light. However she had been sleeping badly and feeling some covert opposition to her business from her family and others.

She brought this dream to a session. It was very vivid and puzzled her. There are two women on a beach. One is attacking the other constantly with a knife. In the end the one being attacked stops defending herself, takes the knife and plunges it into herself.

Clearly two of her inner personalities are in conflict and need to communicate. First I suggested a truce between the two women in the dream so that each could say what they needed to say while the other really listened. They agreed to these terms.

One said. 'I want to do my work. I know it's important – but everyone bothers me. I feel battered. I can't cope and I'm ready to give up.' The other said. 'I'm angry and frightened. She wants to change everything. I know she's right but I want everything to stay as it is'.

The two of them talked for some time, while I helped each to clarify her position, listen to the other and make sure each understood what was going on for the other. Each of them softened gradually as they communicated. They offered safety to each other. Each began to understand the other and at that moment Pam's body gave a convulsive jerk as her heart opened and she sighed. 'They've become one.'

Her dream told her how very much she was threatening herself and how frightened of change she really was. To the extent that she threatened herself in her inner world, as an external manifestation, her family tried to stop her becoming independent.

She phoned me next day to say, she had talked the dream over with her husband and all the work we had done on it. His attitude had changed completely and she had slept like a log.

When we are in conflict internally this will inevitably be marked by external conflict in our lives. When we sort out our inner conflicts, the outer ones melt away.

So where do these sub-personalities come from?

We bring in beliefs and fears with which we haven't dealt in other lives and which we want to understand in this life. Each of these beliefs forms a personality within us.

Most of us are aware that we carry forward into adulthood anything unhealed in childhood, to try to heal. The same principle applies from lifetime to lifetime.

If, for example, we were ill treated in another life and we were still carrying anger and a desire for revenge to the time of our death, that would be an unlearned lesson. We would bring that desire for revenge into this life, which might result in us having a cold, hard, unforgiving streak.

One of our inner personalities would be vengeful, hard and unforgiving.

Perhaps in another lifetime we were cheated by others and the feeling that we wanted to get them back persisted until we died. In that case we would bring in lessons about cheating and quite possibly we will cheat and deceive others. So our inner cheat is born.

A client, Ivor, who was a gentle giant in this life, with an ambivalence about his sexuality, had a deep sense of unworthiness. He created failures in his life because he believed he didn't deserve any good.

When we started to look at his beliefs, he slipped back to the source in another life where he was being put to death for homosexuality. As he waited for death his apathy was evident.

I asked how he was feeling. He kept repeating, 'I deserve to die. I'm bad. I deserve to die.'

Not surprisingly, Ivor brought into this life a whole cluster of inner personalities who believed they were undeserving, bad, unworthy and ought to be punished. He also brought in the ambivalent sexuality to work on.

Because his inner teacher was hyper-critical, it constantly told his 'bad' personalities off and made sure he was punished.

He had many other personalities within his consciousness who were kind, gentle, creative, artistic, nurturing, generous and spiritual. His critical inner teacher devalued these aspects of his nature; we had to lessen the negative impact and allow a wiser, more nurturing teacher to develop within him. Then he began to feel comfortable inside.

When we are ready to resolve our inner conflicts the Universe will bring in people as mirrors for us to look into.

As a child, the only time Sandy was validated by her parents was when she did well at school. So as an adult her aim was for success and recognition. She drove and strove all through her life for recognition. It was her great motivating force.

She had just given a lecture where she had received

much praise, recognition and acclaim. She told me that towards the end of the lecture she had noticed a former colleague in the audience and could feel a strong malevolent energy coming from this person. It ruined Sandy's evening.

When she closed her eyes and visualized the woman, she described her as a witch. 'This witch is horrid. She wants to take me over. Malevolent and nasty . . . ' Sandy shuddered. I asked what the witch needed and Sandy answered promptly, 'Recognition.' She had projected her own need for recognition externally onto this old colleague.

When I asked her to look into the witch's eyes, she described them as horrid and evil. She recognised this as fear and as she looked more deeply into the fear she saw at last a very very frightened child inside the witch. Then she could feel compassion for the witch. At that point the witch said unexpectedly that she could help Sandy.

'How do you feel about letting her help you?' I questioned and Sandy replied that she felt very apprehensive. She was afraid of the unknown.

I explained that there is no fear of the unknown – only memories of fearful things that we have experienced in the past. I asked her to sense the past memory.

She found himself in another life in a female body, being dragged into the darkness. She had been working as a witch and gradually realised to her horror that in the village where she lived all the villagers had banded together against her because they were afraid of her psychic power. Sandy could feel the sense of terror and anger and betrayal as she was tied to the stake and burnt. She could also see the fear in the villagers' eyes.

We did quite a lot more work in her inner world before she was able to feel compassion and understanding for the ignorance and fear of the villagers. Then that witch said, 'I forgive them,' and I could see the flush on Sandy's face as the old energy was released.

Her energy had been trapped in fighting her own inner witch. Now that the Universe had brought her a mirror to look into and she had faced her fear, she could accept that part of herself. That energy is now available to her. And other people with that witch energy can no longer upset her.

No one outside us can upset us. We project a disowned part of us onto them and give them power. The Universe gives us opportunities to look at these disowned parts by bringing mirrors into our lives for us to look into.

So if we dislike something in someone else or are afraid of them, then it is up to us to look at ourselves in the mirror they hold up.

It is only where there is a body shift, such as a twitch, a change of colour, or breathing that we know a healing has taken place in the emotional body. This transfers to the physical and our energy flows where it was previously blocked.

Carole had a deep belief that she didn't deserve anything good to happen. All her life she had created illness after illness, and depression, so she was blocking much of her available energy. Within her consciousness, her personalities were in conflict. The deeply undeserving one was bitter and hurting. At the same time she had an extremely intuitive, aware side to her.

One day she brought a fragment of a dream about a horrible shrivelled old woman and a beautiful young girl. She closed her eyes to picture them and said she was both of them. I asked her to see the horrible shrivelled old woman first and really recognise her. She did this and could connect with that side of her personality.

Carole became the old, shrivelled woman. At that instant she was shocked to see on her inner screen the beautiful young girl appear. A warrior rode into her picture and ran a sword through the young girl.

Carole immediately realized she was seeing another life where the young woman was her daughter. She seemed to shrink in the chair as she re-experienced this old horror. She physically felt her heart exploding and poured curses onto the warrior. Her daughter was dead. All that she loved was taken from her. She was alone. Now that his wife was dead, her daughter's husband never visited her. She felt very lonely but she never expressed it. She just shut herself away and continued until her death to curse and hate the man who killed her daughter.

And now centuries later, in visualisation, she told her then son in-law that she was lonely and that she missed having a man around the place. She asked him to visit. To her surprise, he replied, 'I enjoy coming to see you when I can. I regard this as home but I feel unwanted.' He wanted to visit her! This was his home! Carole felt a shift in her heart.

Then she spoke to the warrior who had killed her daughter. She felt a new understanding and freely lifted the curse she had put on him. She felt her heart open and her face become suffused with a rosy glow.

At that she felt herself rising and floating and being drawn into space to a new level, higher than anything she had ever experienced. A Light figure came in and talked to her, telling her that her suffering was over. She must stop worrying and believe and walk in the Light. Awareness and forgiveness had integrated her conflicting personalities, healing the past life as well as this one. Those past life personalities could no longer run her.

She opened her eyes looking radiant and alive. Love had opened up her energy channels.

ELEVEN

Healing Hurts

Every person in our lives has been placed there by the Universe to show us about our inner personalities and how we deal with them. When we look at the people in our lives it is like looking into a mirror. As we see how we respond to them, we can learn an enormous amount about ourselves.

I hadn't seen Margaret for some months. She had started a new job and was very involved with it. She told me that she was enjoying the job though she was taking work home and suffering from headaches. She said the staff were being demanding and seemed to need her attention.

When people are demanding of us, we are often not listening to our own needs. In order that we can see this more clearly, we attract in demanding people as a mirror to look into.

I asked Margaret to tell me about the staff. She started with a young school leaver of seventeen who had said to her, 'I feel as if you don't have time for me.'

I asked her to close her eyes and relax. She immediately saw the seventeen year old, who came up to her.

'Ask her what she wants,' I directed.

Margaret did this. 'I want you to show interest,' the young woman said.

I asked Margaret to see herself as she was at seventeen. 'What do you need?' I questioned.

'I want someone to have time for me and show an interest in me,' she said promptly. 'I need to be shown I'm appreciated and for someone to look at what I'm doing.'

The mirror was becoming clearer.

I asked the wise adult part of Margaret to take an interest in what the seventeen year old part of her was doing. She spent some time in her inner world experiencing this and feeling the comfort of it. Then she volunteered that when she was appreciated she didn't need headaches.

She accepted the lesson that she must find time for herself and appreciate and take an interest in herself, and then we moved on to look in the next mirror.

Another member of staff came into her inner picture. 'She moans all the time,' Margaret told me. 'She always feels she's hard done by.' I feel really cross with her.

I suggested she go back into a time in her life when she felt hard done by. I knew that she would either be moaning herself (a direct reflection of the staff member) or would have to suppress the moaning and react in some other way.

'I'm fourteen. I'm angry because I want things like the other kids. I'm afraid that if I can't be like them, they won't like me.'

Again we brought in the wise woman who talked to Margaret and helped her to open her heart. As the fourteen year old opened her heart, she saw a radiant yellow and pink light surround her. Then she could mingle with the other children and just be herself. They all liked and accepted her.

Evidently she had not been allowed to moan so she had suppressed this and become angry instead. No wonder she felt cross with the staff member, who was doing what she couldn't allow herself to do.

I asked who told her she must not moan. 'Grandma. She says people don't like moaners.' She instantly saw herself become five years old as her grandmother talked to her. Now she was able to tell her grandma what she needed. 'I need to be like the other children, because I'm afraid I won't be accepted if I'm different.'

The wise woman came in again and gave her confidence and love. Margaret felt her inner five year old become golden and happy. She could easily play amongst her classmates. She knew that this small child didn't need headaches.

Margaret was quite curious now about what the other staff members could tell her about herself. One of them came in. 'She's always asking questions, even when she knows the answers. It's very irritating,' Margaret told me. Then, without further prompting, she added, 'She needs re-assurance all the time. I'm a bit short with her.'

In her visualisation she gave the woman the re-assurance and understanding that she craved. As she did this she watched the woman's confidence grow, so that she didn't need to keep asking questions. She realized how counter productive being short with her had been.

Having looked at the mirror, Margaret looked at herself and realized how much re-assurance she needed and how hard on herself she was all the time. She clearly saw how counter productive this was for her.

We brought in the wise woman again. She was, of course, one of Margaret's inner personalities whom she needed to develop. The wise woman was able to give her sensible counsel which made her feel more confident.

When we talked about what she had experienced, Margaret was clearly amazed at how much she learnt about herself from the people she had attracted into her life. She knew that now she was developing her wise inner personality and was treating herself differently, she would automatically treat the staff at work differently and the situation at work would change. It did.

We all have a wise inner personality. Very often we can imagine a wise grandmother or particularly wonderful uncle and listen to them giving us advice.

The inner and the outer are the same. That energy is both within us and can be an entity outside us.

When we have deeply ingrained guilt feelings, we continue to punish ourselves because we feel we are bad and are expecting God to punish us. So we are naturally attracted to a religion with a punitive philosophy. At an intellectual level we know that a loving God never punishes, but at an unconscious level we hold a belief in badness deserving punishment and retribution.

Guilt is often described as a way of not taking responsibility. As long as we feel guilty about being alive, we don't take responsibility for making sure we enjoy life. As long as we feel guilty about our sexuality, we are not taking responsibility for enjoying it. How can we enjoy being a mother when we feel guilty about ourselves as a woman?

Guilt is an emotion to warn us that we are doing something inconsistent with our true values. So when we feel guilt, we need to assess our values, forgive our past behaviour which helped us to learn – and make changes. Then we are taking responsibility for ourselves. Then guilt has served its constructive purpose.

Guilt is sometimes called resentment turned inwards. Very often we feel resentment towards someone or something. If we cannot express it because we believe we are bad, then we may turn it inward against ourselves. Then it becomes guilt. As it becomes safe to acknowledge and express our underlying resentment, the guilt begins to dissolve.

John felt terribly guilty about the women he had slept with before he was married. He had been brought up as a Roman Catholic; and his mother was a punitive, frigid repressed person who had taught him that sex outside marriage was bad. Not surprisingly his father had left home years before.

So John, in his seeking for love, slept with many women. Like many, he had received such confused messages about love and sex that he equated sex with love. Each time he had sex he felt overpowering guilt. When we looked under the guilt, he felt such resentment towards his mother and God that he felt murderous.

I asked him to close his eyes and imagine an animal which represented the guilt he felt. A sly fox appeared and attacked a whole lot of chickens and snapped their heads off. Then a farmer came out and beat the fox to death. The clarity of his visualization showed him what he was constantly doing to himself and women. He realized how much resentment he bore towards his mother, which he deflected through sex onto women – he snapped the heads off the chicken. Then he beat himself to death with guilt.

I asked him to bring the fox to life and take time to listen to its needs. When he heard how desperately alone the fox felt and how much it wanted to be accepted and loved, John broke down and cried and cried. The tears started to wash away the guilt and resentment. Over the next few weeks he continued to wash away the negative beliefs towards his mother. That meant he could accept his sexuality. Now he is married with two small sons and is breaking the chain of guilt which has passed down the family for generations.

All of us who are working to understand and heal ourselves are offering a gift to past generations as well as to future ones.

Miranda still couldn't get over the fact that she had had an abortion years before she was married, when she was a teenager. She had really wanted the baby and held a lot of anger towards her mother who insisted that she have the abortion. When she was eighteen her mother had seemed all powerful and yet she felt guilty that she had not stood up to her and kept the baby. She felt that the soul had wanted to be born to her particularly and she had somehow let it down.

There was also a part of her which recognised that the timing was wrong and if that soul was really serious about having her for a mother, it would have tried again at a more suitable time.

It felt important to help Miranda to connect with the energy of that child so I helped her to relax and go to a higher level where she could meet her aborted child. She saw him quite quickly. He was a teenager himself now. Miranda described what was happening aloud. 'He's holding his arms out to me. He's saying, "I love you. I just needed to be near you."'

Miranda said to him, 'I'm sorry if I held you back by not letting you be born.'

'Oh no. I want to be here,' he reassured her. 'But I wanted to make the connection with you.

She told him that she hadn't wanted to lose him. 'I was frightened of my mother but I wanted you so very much.' He told her his name and that he totally understood and loved her very much. Also that he was always close to her.

I suggested that Miranda now bring in a wise person who could start a programme of healing for the teenage Miranda who had to let go of her baby. Miranda brought in her great-aunt, who told her to relax. The great-aunt said, 'It's time for you to understand. He chose to stay in spirit. It's time for you to let him go. You must promise him that you won't hold him back from growing.'

Miranda started to cry again, 'But I need to be near him.' I asked her how long she needed to hold the child in order to heal her pain. She asked for six months of holding him close to fill the emptiness inside her. In her inner world she held him close to her for six months until there was only a quiet accepting love inside her.

After several minutes her whole body relaxed. Then her great-aunt told her that it had all been planned at a higher level and she was not to look back any more. All this happened at a spiritual level, with her great-aunt in spirit and her child in spirit. At the same time, it was within Miranda. She held a lost child personality and a wise great-aunt personality in her psyche and this work did something to integrate her inner lost child and strengthen her wise inner great-aunt.

Linear time is an illusion. In trance we can condense or expand time. So we can experience and heal a whole lifetime of hurt in moments . . . and we can make a moment of joy last for years.

Sometimes we find we behave differently with one friend or colleague or even family member from the way we normally do with others. Of course those particular people are triggering one of our inner personalities which usually lies dormant.

Chrissy had come through an emotionally deprived childhood. She had been depressed and sad and powerless for many years. She had done an enormous amount of personal development work and had integrated much of this depressed personality. She was mostly very capable and strong. She said to me that she couldn't understand why she always felt tired and depressed with her eldest daughter. It was her daughter who provided the clue to understanding what was taking place between them.

Her daughter realized that she, as the oldest girl, had always been given the message from Daddy to keep Mummy happy. So the child took on the task of keeping her depressed mother happy. The child became programmed with, 'I have to keep Mum happy.' Chrissy, her mother, colluded with the child and took in the belief, 'This child has to support me and make me happy.' Consequently whenever Chrissy and her daughter met they activated their programming. So she collapsed and became depressed and helpless and her daughter supported her.

As soon as Chrissy became aware of her part in the collusion, she talked it through with her daughter and they worked together to change their relationship.

The greatest gift we can give anyone is to hold up the mirror of their own perfection for them to look at.

TWELVE

Victim and Rescuer

Most of us have a victim in our class of inner personalities. When we are victims we believe we are at the whim of others and of fate. We feel powerless to help ourselves and feel very hurt and vulnerable inside. And of course we blame other people and fate for what's happening to us.

Being a victim is a common survival strategy. We attract helpers and get plenty of attention, often negative, but nevertheless attention. The victim receives advice and help from anyone he can hook in. He has, of course, no intention of taking the advice or help, because that would end the game. If the helper has a particularly strong pleaser, he can be hooked for years trying to get it right for the victim.

Because it is too painful to look at our own hurting parts, many people try instead to help others. This way we can feel worthwhile and powerful without taking responsibility for healing our own hurts.

Many victims become rescuers. Rescuing others gives us the illusion we are in control of our lives.

Rescuers have an investment in keeping the victim dependent. After all, if the drowning man learns to swim, he won't need to be rescued any more. For every victim there is a rescuer disempowering him. If we save someone from drowning and teach him to swim, that empowers him. When we empower other people we light a light in them.

People occasionally phone and ask me to help their partners or children to change. They say their lives would be great if only the other person would be different. That is victim consciousness.

We can't expect anyone else to change. We can only change ourselves. When we take mastery we take responsibility for our own lives. Then we accept we attracted or created that relationship and when we change ourselves, the relationship will change. Giving advice is always rescuing. If we give someone advice which they take and something unfortunate occurs, then we bear part of the karma.

Victims and rescuers set up games between themselves to keep themselves stuck and get their needs met.

Andrew was a very sensitive, kindly man who was never quite in control of his life and was often depressed and miserable. He frequently had flu at the weekend. His wife rallied round and nursed him and encouraged him and they would moan about the awful dangerous world out there. Then it would be her turn to become depressed and unable to cope and he would rescue her.

So they set up a game, taking it in turns to be a victim! The breakthrough came when his wife acknowledged that she was angry with Andrew. As she hesitantly expressed her anger, she realised that she didn't have to support him in his addiction to being a victim.

That Friday she arrived home from work to find Andrew in bed with flu and feeling very sorry for himself. Instead of going into her old pattern of cancelling her weekend arrangements and providing him with hot drinks and sympathy, she expressed her anger and frustration and told him she was going out. To the surprise of both of them, by the following day his flu was better and his spirits rose. The payoff had been taken away from him. The victim game was over. Both Andrew and his wife felt much stronger.

Rescuers are invariably pleasers. When as children, we feel very vulnerable inside, we try to protect ourselves. Depending on what happened to us in other lives, we often try to protect our vulnerable inner child by pleasing others. That way we will always have someone to love us.

While our inner pleaser is balanced this works well, for we are charming and genuinely interested in others. But if as a small child, we try harder and harder to please others and perhaps still get criticised or feel unloved, then we stop being balanced. We become overpleasing. Then we are ready to do anything for anyone, to be a martyr, just as long as we keep people liking us – or dependent on us. The more effort we put into pleasing, the more we bury the resentment, the anger, the demanding and needy parts of ourselves. The more we bury and deny, the more phony we become and people don't really trust us. Somewhere they sense the resentment and neediness behind all that we do for them – and they are afraid it will burst out and envelop or trap them.

Rosie was a classic rescuer-cum-pleaser and very needy. Her father abandoned her mother when she was quite small. He re-appeared in her teens with a new wife and daughter. This daughter he adored. He refused to acknowledge Rosie as his daughter. To disguise the rage and pain and frustration she felt, Rosie tried to please men. She charmed them close to her but, when they were close, the needy, hurting side would emerge. Then they would soon back off.

She married once but her husband abandoned her soon after their child was born. After that she only rescued unhappily married men. In each case the wife kept her from her man just as effectively as her half sister had kept her from her father.

When we are afraid of being abandoned, we need to keep people dependent on us and, of course, Rosie was no exception. She made herself indispensable to her daughter. She hung onto her by making the nest so comfortable that she couldn't leave. She did everything for her . . . and burned with resentment.

Rosie's rescuer was in full swing in one session. She arrived seething. She was furiously angry with her neighbour. This neighbour had an eighteen year old daughter called Martine. When Martine went to college, her neighbour took in a lodger, so that there was no room for Martine

when she wanted to come home one weekend. Rosie felt
Martine's pain so acutely that she phoned her neighbour in
the middle of the night and they quarrelled about it.

When I asked Rosie what had happened for her at the
age of eighteen, Martine's age, and how she was feeling
then, she used almost the same words as she had done to
describe Martine's feelings (as she imagined them).

It was only when I fed this back to her that she realized
that she was seeing outside herself the mirror of unhealed
pain which was inside her. She could rescue a thousand
Martines without ever healing her own pain. And she
couldn't help Martine without healing herself first.

In time she realised that she could rescue a thousand
unhappily married men without healing her own pain. She
recognised that as a child she had had to develop her
pleaser to protect herself and get recognition. Rosie worked
to fill her inner void with self-love and worth. Then we
worked to strengthen the wise inner teacher and the
nurturing parent who could now protect her inner child
and give her a sense of value. She began to let go of the
compulsion to please and care for others and start to value
herself.

Here is a typical example of how a rescuer, his name was
Harry, stopped others from being free to sort out their own
problems. Harry was a delightful, charming man with an
infectious boyish enthusiasm. Today, however, he looked
very earnest as he explained just how much he wanted to
help his wife, Jo, to move from her stuck position. He
wanted Jo to share his experiences of self discovery and his
new lightness. 'I want her to fly with me,' he said.

Jo and her best friend Violet had quarrelled. Harry could
see both sides and tried to help each of them understand
the other's situation. He went from one to the other of them
trying to make it better. This was of course his pattern. As a
child he had anxiously tried to make it better between his
parents.

I asked him to close his eyes and visualise what was
happening. He saw Jo and Violet standing there while he,
Harry, was a small boy running between them imploring

them to be friends. I asked him to leave them and fly off into the Universe on his own. After a time he came back and saw that the two women had come together but still weren't talking. I suggested he ignore them and fly off and explore the Universe some more on his own.

This time when he returned they were friends and staring up at him. He waved and disappeared off again. When he came back the two women had lifted themselves up and were both tentatively learning to fly. He went off several more times to enjoy the Universe and each time the two friends were flying higher and freer. When he finally reluctantly opened his eyes Harry knew that he could never help his wife by joining in her misery.

And in reality, as he let go of being the rescuer/go-between, the two women did make it up. And his wife, Jo, started to take an interest in self development work.

When we take responsibility for ourselves and leave others free, everyone has a chance to grow.

It is possible for all of us to work on ourselves to heal our own inner victim.

This is an example of how I work on my lessons. It may only seem a little one, but for me the feeling involved is very real and I realised as I wrote this how this feeling has disrupted my life. My husband and I were on holiday in France and the alarm clock went off very early, waking me and making me jump. I assumed it had been accidentally set, but to my surprise my husband got out of bed and dressed. He is a big man and incapable of doing this quietly! Then he crept out of the bedroom.

My thoughts started whirling. How dare he set the alarm without telling me? He's gone off and left me. He's doing something without me. I'm left out. My stomach clenched tight with anger and I practised a few choice sarcastic expressions about non-communication and non-sharing to use on him over breakfast.

That of course was my old victim pattern rearing its ugly head. I realise by now that I have choices. So, perceiving my blaming, attacking, angry feelings, I recognised a lesson coming to find me. I lay back in the pillow and quietened my mind. Up came past pictures. When I was pregnant and on bedrest, my first husband was at a party. I was alone, having contractions, while he was having fun. I felt abandoned. Instead of phoning and asking him to come home, I seethed and took it out on him when he did come home.

I could go back and back in my life with this feeling and eventually saw myself as a small girl, just over a year old, with a new brother. This was the precious boy, the son, and my parents were playing with this baby. And I was alone and angry. I could sense myself toddling into the room, cross, disruptive, needy, demanding and getting rejected.

Now in my inner scene I could smile and let my wise adult self show my toddler self the truth, that she was loved and wanted. When my toddler felt safe and secure and loved, I could change my inner scene and watch myself run into the room where my parents were playing with my baby brother, this time smiling, laughing, light, knowing they were all delighted to see me and saw their faces light up as the small happy toddler ran in.

I smiled and felt more comfortable as I snuggled deeper into the pillow. I had been playing out the illusion a long time. Of course, the real lovable me was wanted and I could choose the way I played the breakfast scenario – in the old victim way, with anger and hurt and recrimination or with love and interest about where my husband had gone.

My logical mind knew anyway that he had crept out to walk in the woods. Now I could start to take responsibility. How had I created it that he didn't want to share the walk with me? I remembered that he had been quiet the evening before and I had barely noticed when he had gone off to have a bath while I was busy chatting with other people.

So perhaps I or someone else had done something to upset him and press his buttons. That was clearly his problem and at the same time I could easily sense his hurt and be happy to nourish him, now that I had nourished my hurt toddler. I dressed and went out to look for him. I found him in the woods and we went into breakfast together. I heard about all he had seen. I no longer felt needy and demanding. He soon felt safe enough to tell me what it was that had upset him so that he had needed space to go off alone, and we were able to discuss it. Then I could validate his feelings to help his healing.

So when we have an over the top angry victim feeling, the steps are:

1. Identify the feeling. Do you feel used, abandoned, resentful, misunderstood, hurt etc.?
2. Sense the first time this was triggered in childhood.
3. Open your heart and change and heal that scene. This fills that well of neediness and opens up choices to respond differently.
4. See what choices you have to respond differently.
5. Clearly see yourself responding in a different way.
6. Do it.

Each time we choose to respond differently we are putting new messages into our unconscious mind, enabling us to take mastery choices.

THIRTEEN

Our Shadow Self

So often it is the quiet, repressed person who has the unexpected violent outburst, with devastating consequences. It is the too-good-to-be-true, virtuous, pious preacher who has the damaging affair.

Within our consciousness it is the personalities we push down and ignore and refuse to recognise which burst out and severely embarrass us. And because we have suppressed them we often don't know how to recognise them.

So how do we recognise our suppressed parts.

1. Anything we suppress is drawn to our attention in dreams.
2. Any person we dislike is showing us a personality within ourself that we dislike. If we positively hate someone, then we have that hated personality suppressed within us.
3. When we have extreme responses to something, there is something not dealt with inside us.

So if we are in a safe, dull marriage and we dream of wild animals trying to get out of a cage, we need to start looking at what the wild animal within us needs and to liven up our relationship. Otherwise the wild animal personality will burst out and cause problems in our marriage. If we dream of a powerless animal trying to bite us, we need to look at how the powerless bit of us gets its own back.

Maybe we nag or control or manipulate in an inappropriate way and we are hurting ourselves with it (biting ourselves) with guilt or put-downs.

Whatever we do to ourselves we do to others.

Sonia's parents had a stormy relationship, each constantly struggling for power. Her mother was very domineering and at the same time frightened and demanding. Not surprisingly, Sonia too had two conflicting inner personalities. She swung from being powerful and in control to being needy and demanding. Of course, she attracted a partner who fitted nicely into her pattern. When she was needy and demanding he became authoritarian and punitive. When she became powerful and in control, he chased her and followed her everywhere.

She had just swung again from the powerfully in control phase to the needy, demanding phase when she came to see me. And a few days before she had had a dream which introduced her to her conflicting personalities.

In the dream she was walking down a path which she thought was safe, but there on the right hand side of the path appeared a man. He had dark, unkept hair and a knife in his hand. She felt powerless, frightened and betrayed because she was sure this path was safe. She knew that the man represented her masculine energy and the fact that he was standing on the right confirmed this.

She was quite eager to go into the dream and face him. Because he was such a sinister, frightening figure, I asked her if she wanted a screen between them or someone to be with her, but she said no. She knew she was safe and in control of her inner scene now.

She closed her eyes and conjured up the dream. The man was just standing there waiting for her and when she asked him what he wanted, he told her he wanted to hurt her. She asked why and he said he was angry because he felt defenceless and he didn't think anyone cared about him.

I asked Sonia to check with the man if anyone did care and he said that they did but when he felt no one cared, he wanted to hurt someone and he picked on her because she was vulnerable.

'How can he deal with his feelings?' I enquired via Sonia.

'He can get his anger out and that will help. He's afraid

that he is inadequate and he has nothing to give.' She paused to think and then she told him that he only needed to be himself. The man said he didn't believe it. His mother always wanted things from him.

The man watched while Sonia invited her mother into the scene. As soon as she saw her, Sonia turned into a child. She recalled how her mother always wanted things and she could never provide them and so could never make her mother happy. Now, as that child, she told her mother how inadequate she felt because she couldn't give her things. Her mother said she only wanted Sonia to love her – but the child couldn't believe this any more than the man had done.

We brought in a role model of someone who was a good wise mother. Sonia immediately brightened. 'She says I'm strong and the only thing I need to give is love. I believe it when she tells me.' Sonia now told her mother that she couldn't give her anything but she loved her. Her mother smiled and, for the first time ever, Sonia knew that was enough.

'I don't have to give things in order to be loved,' she murmured and was able to grow up into an adult again. It was like letting a burden go. She could feel the glow of this release in every part of her body.

She went over to the man in the dream. He was sitting now quietly watching, no longer threatening. They sat comfortably together by the fire. Sonia's dream told her that whenever she felt no one cared, she became dangerous. To be more accurate, in her inner world whenever her feminine aspect felt vulnerable and uncared for, her masculine aspect would become dangerous and attack.

What she did internally, she did externally in her relationship. She really listened to the message about her inner personalities and started to understand what happened when they were in conflict.

She started talking to the good wise mother each day. This good wise mother was as much an inner personality as her inner demanding mother. It was time she gave the good wise mother more time and energy.

Remembering the wonderful comfort of the fire and the togetherness of her two personalities by it, she started to affirm

> I feel comfy and strong
> For now I belong.

The second way of recognising our shadows is to look at the people we are in conflict with.

Where there is conflict outside us, there is corresponding conflict within us.

Where there is peace within, there is peace in our outer world.

Judy was always on the go. She never sat down to relax. As a mother of four, there was plenty to do. No she never read a book during the day. She couldn't bring herself to do that. As a child she was always the one who helped her mother and that was where she received her validation as a daughter, a very common pattern.

Her strongest inner personalities were those who were caring, responsible, nurturing of others and always hard working.

As so often happens with children, her daughter was her greatest teacher. Judy described her daughter as lazy. She simply couldn't understand why she lay in bed all day. She couldn't fathom why the girl didn't study for exams. She was perplexed and bewildered and angry at her daughter's behaviour. Of course, the child was showing Judy her shadow self. The behaviour that Judy had never allowed herself to indulge in and had severely repressed, was being held up as a mirror by her daughter.

When Judy realized this she started giving herself permission to relax and let the playful, carefree personality within her come out and grow.

When we balance ourselves out, in a subtle and incredible way this touches others and gives them permission to balance too. To Judy's amazement, her daughter found herself a job and started to study in her spare time.

So many of us like to appear to be together, nice and in command of life. On the surface we are pleasant and happy while the shadow personality within feels used and abused. This used, abused part of us is not acknowledged or heard and if triggered an eruption may occur. These extreme reactions warn us of the presence of one of our shadow personalities.

Wendy had done a great deal of spiritual growth work and was very aware of many of her personalities. On this particular day she looked very upset and wanted to talk about a row she had had with her husband, which seemed so trivial on the surface.

The actual altercation started because he had made himself a cup of tea and hadn't made her one. 'It's so trivial, I'm ashamed to mention it,' she confessed. 'And yet I felt angry, hurt, frustrated, powerless. My throat went and my mouth felt dry.' Nothing is trivial if we feel such an extreme response. The not making of a cup of tea for her was merely a trigger for deeper things.

I suggested she focus on those same physical and emotional feelings and bring pictures to mind of where they came from. She felt herself as a child having her tonsils out. She wanted her mother. No one came and she couldn't scream. She had the same awful feeling of a dry mouth and hurting throat. She felt caged in and powerless and started to shake.

I encouraged her to go more deeply into those feelings and suddenly she was in a horrendous past life where she had been a young virtuous girl who was abducted and shipped overseas in a cage. There she was sold as a slave girl into a brothel. She shook with sobs as she described how she was used and abused by men. She was powerless to escape or say anything. It went on for years and years. Her shoulders slumped. 'Years and years of it and nothing I could do.' She screamed suddenly with an outpouring of buried rage.

'I'm in my forties now. I'm broken and ill. A nun comes and takes me away and cares for me. I die of exhaustion. After all I've gone through, just when I'm rescued, I die of sheer exhaustion. It's too late.' She shivered. She wanted to stay with the nun. She identified so much with the love and peace and healing radiated by this gentle person. It felt too much that now she had found her, she died. She left her body reluctantly.

That particular day, not being made a cup of tea triggered the deeply suppressed feelings of being used and abused by men. It reminded her of being treated as a thing, not as an honoured person. Because in this life she identified so much with the nun, who was respected and honoured for her spirituality, she buried the shadow personality of the woman used and abused by men. And that lurking shadow self had an over-the-top reaction from time to time.

Now it was time to cast light on the shadow self and bring it into the light. She looked down on that life and saw them all . . . all those men who had abused her in that life . . . as a great black ball of men. 'There's a huge cord from that ball of men to my sexual organs. I'm starting to cut it with a saw. It is taking ages.'

I waited a long time while she completed this cutting. She was sobbing. 'Those men are wolves and beasts. I want to shoot them all . . . and take them out to sea . . . and drown them.' She did this with gusto. I suggested she allow a gentle, caring, shining man to emerge from the sea, a man who honoured her. She did this and let him take the other end of the cord from her abdomen.

When I suggested that she allow him to honour her body in whatever way she wanted, she became quiet for a long time. Then she told me she was breathing in the new sensation of being honoured. After a while, she said quietly and gently, 'The shining man out of the sea has turned into my husband.' The used and abused part of her was healing. A deep wound in her psyche was cleansed. The nun and the whore were being integrated.

FOURTEEN

Past Lives

I remember the moment when someone first explained to me that we all have many lives and go from one experience to another to grow and learn. She told me that if we cheat in one life, someone will cheat us in another. If we hurt people, we will have an urge to repay what we did by healing or helping those people. If we maim someone we may choose to have a limp in this life to experience what it felt like to have that done to us.

It was as, if in one flash, everything made sense. The Law of Karma, which is the Law of Cause and Effect over lifetimes, struck a chord of knowing within me.

As soon as I understood and accepted this it opened something up within me, for I started to attract people into my life who had an intuitive feeling for past lives. I sat next to a man on a course and he turned to me and said, 'Hallo. We were in a Greek life together,' and there was an 'Ah yes!' response within me. This started to happen more often.

One day I was luxuriating in a warm bath. Suddenly a voice deep in my head said, 'Nancy was your mother.' Nancy was a client I felt close to. It was like a thunderclap in my head and I jumped out of the bath in shock. Although I totally accepted the information I set out to verify it by asking a well known channel, who confirmed that Nancy had been my mother in another life.

Nowadays I accept these messages and promptings from unseen forces. In those early days I ran to all sorts of people for validation. In the course of time my awareness deepened until I had flashes, knowings or whole scenes of my past life experiences. Again in those early days I would blurt out my impressions. Luckily spirit protects the innocent.

I remember staying at a centre for a few days. The only other person staying there was a very old lady. We spoke briefly and I knew I already knew her. The feeling was very strong. I went for a walk alone and realized we had been in Egypt together. Over supper I told her that I felt we had been together before. She smiled sweetly and said,'I'm so glad you recognised me, my dear. We were temple sisters together in Egypt.' She then proceeded to tell me fascinating stories of our time together. I later discovered she had been a well known medium.

With the raising of energy on the planet more and more of us are having past life flashes and awarenesses and are becoming interested in exploring past lives to understand and heal ourselves at a deeper level.

Our past lives have an enormous impact on our current one. Our past ten lives have the same relevance to this life as the past ten years have to this year. We are all products of our past experiences.

If we are reading chapter ten in a book, it aids our understanding of situations and characters to read the earlier chapters. Just as looking at the patterns we are repeating in this life helps us to change them, so when we look at past lives, we can stop the patterns by awareness, by understanding and by forgiveness.

I believe that looking at our past lives assists our journey to wholeness.

It is important to realize that when we are afraid, we are not imagining the future, we are re-living the distant past.

We cannot fear something we have never experienced.

So if we fear abandonment by our partner, we will sometime have been abandoned and have retained the trace memory in our consciousness. By the Laws of the Universe whatever we fear we attract into our lives, so that we can re-experience it in our effort to overcome it. So we can continue with the same experiences, lifetime after lifetime in our effort to learn what we need to know.

I have often found thats when clients have had sessions in which they have seen several past lives all on the same theme as their current one, they look quite shaken. Usually they say, 'Well I don't want to do all that again. I'm going to stop doing that now.'

Julian was a very overprotective father. This is quite unusual in itself. It is usually the mother who is overprotective but in this case Julian could hardly trust his wife to look after the two children. He was petrified of something happening to them. His attitudes were beginning to undermine the marriage.

It was only when he went back into other lives that he understood the reason for this. In one he had been very careless and thoughtless. He had been more interested in winning a business contract than in the children. When he had undertaken to look after them, he left them alone and they had died in a fire.

In another, in a female life, he was the mother of the same two children. They had died in an accident. As their mother she blamed herself. In yet another, one of the children had fallen into a fast flowing river. This time she was the child's aunt. She had desperately tried to save him but they both drowned.

In his inner world, while tuned into his inner wisdom, Julian realized that in those other lifetimes it was his desperate fear for their safety which had attracted the disasters. At a deep core level he recognised that this time it could be different. He became aware that his time he must offer them a framework of safety and yet at the same time the freedom to explore. Then he must hand them over to divine protection and trust they would be safe.

During these sessions Julian had released a lot of guilt and anguish, forgiven himself for his past carelessness and was ready to release his tight control on his children. For the first time he started to feel confidence in himself as a father. His relationship with his wife improved as he let go of his grip on the children. Her confidence in herself as a mother began to improve too.

So, looking at past lives puts our fears into context, so that we get a new perspective on our lives.

When we see how we carry on difficulties with certain people from lifetime to lifetime, we have a great incentive to change for ever. We incarnate again and again with the same people to try to get an understanding. In one lifetime that person may be our aunt, in another our son, then our father, then brother – every possible combination – but we repeat the same pattern.

The moment we are ready the Universe will present us with the perfect opportunities and people to help us make the awarenesses and shifts we need.

Brian was in a power struggle with his sister over who was going to look after their very sick, elderly mother. They both wanted to. Both wanted to take the decisions for her care. Both wanted to look after her finances. They lived at opposite ends of the country. They fought and argued on the phone and nothing was resolved. In the meantime the mother they were fighting over was in a home.

Brian was convinced his sister didn't have his mother's best interests at heart. However, when he looked at the past lives with his sister, he found they had been brothers together as well as father and son. The common theme was that they had always been at war over someone or something. Each thought he was right and the other had false motives.

From a higher perspective Brian saw that in each case if one of them had let go everything would have been all right. Something shifted in him. He saw the fruitlessness of the continual power struggle. He tried to understand his sister's feelings for her mother and began to acknowledge that she did love their mother and want the best for her.

He let go. He trusted that in doing so the best interests of his mother would be served. He told his sister that he felt she could take good care of his mother. He felt a release in his body and he started to feel warm towards his sister. Through awareness and love he ended lifetimes of power struggle. He is now setting up a good relationship with his sister for their next life together.

If someone hurts us and we bear anger and unforgiveness towards them, we may choose to experience what was going on for them when they hurt us. This is so that our soul can understand them and find compassion and oneness.

This is how I found within me one little piece of compassion for someone I had been judging at a deep, unconscious, unaware level. From much work that I had done, I knew that I had put invisible shutters up against my mother at birth. At that moment of soul recognition I had had a past life memory of rejection.

Two years before, in meditation, I had contacted a deep feeling of shock and fear as my mother, in an Indian life, threw me into a lake to drown me. I was a small girl and as she threw me, she shouted, 'It's only a girl'.

She was my mother then as she is now. It is not surprising then that I chose for this life to be born in India where girls are not valued and into a family where women are de-valued.

On this particular evening a group of us sat round our dining room table and wrote for five hours every thought which came into our heads. The purpose of this is to let go of the critical censor and become aware of how we are creating karma with our thoughts. It is a powerful exercise, as I found.

After two or three hours of writing, I found myself in that same life and this time the story flowed from my pen. As I connected with this memory again I became aware of the fact that I, as that little girl, was handicapped in some way and was a hindrance to the tribe. I could feel that my mother was heartbroken to drown me but felt she had no option for the sake of the tribe. The only way she could rationalise her actions was by thinking I was only a girl. I was very aware of her grief. Despite her grief and my intellectual understanding, I felt no compassion. I could feel four solid lumps of anger in my heart centre.

As I wrote, I became aware of other connections. One of my daughters had meningitis when small and we were told she was severely mentally retarded. I felt the family couldn't cope with this and, during the long desperate hours of that first day, I remember the thought coming in that I'd have to suffocate her, for the sake of everyone else. As my pen flowed on I felt the pain of my own grief at these memories because I had such a bonding of love with this child.

(This thought was never put to the test as she made a complete miraculous recovery, as described in *Light Up Your Life*.)

I now realize that I had this experience to help me understand what my mother had felt obliged to do to me in that Indian life, and so find compassion and forgiveness within me. Even when I stopped writing and the story stopped flowing through my mind, I could still feel the solid hard lumps of unforgiveness in my heart. I meditated and tried to release it but the tell-tale unyielding lumps in my chest revealed the truth. I was still unforgiving.

I was quite angry and impatient with myself. At an intellectual level I wanted to forgive but my body still held onto the hurt. I knew I couldn't force forgiveness, so every night before sleep I prayed for help to find forgiveness and grace for my mother and to release myself. This continued for three weeks and then I had an amazing dream about my mother and woke with a tremendous feeling of compassion and love for her. My heart felt warm and soft. At last something had dissolved within me.

FIFTEEN

The Body Remembers

In the centre of every cell of our body is a divine flame. When we are totally happy, flowing and relaxed, the divine wisdom in the centre of each cell is available and we enjoy good health.

The only thing that can imprison the divine flame in each cell is fear. All anger, hurt, criticism, jealousy and negative thoughts are fears. They cause us to tense up parts of our body so that the divine wisdom is blocked and unavailable to us. As soon as we open up and release the tension, with love, forgiveness, compassion or awareness and understanding, divine energy flows and we are healed.

Our cells are constantly dying and being replaced. In seven years every cell of our body has been renewed, so we have the possibility of totally transforming our body, at least within seven years. The reason we don't heal is because we hold onto old painful memories. When we suppress we hold on, so any emotional or physical pain which we suppress, we sustain in our unconscious minds and in the cellular memory of our bodies.

So if someone falls and cuts his foot, he cuts it in that particular place in that particular way because of something he holds in his consciousness at that time. As long as he holds that particular belief in his mind, the scar will remain. When he dissolves the cause, the scar will heal. Unacknowledged and unexpressed emotional pain carried over lifetimes eventually crystalises into something physical.

Moment by moment we build our bodies. Belief by belief

we build our bone structure. Thought by thought we put flesh on our structure. Emotion by emotion we create the fluid systems in our body.

And as we construct our bodies, we construct the weaknesses, the misalignments, the fat, the illnesses.

When we build something we don't like into our bodies it is offering us an opportunity for awareness. Every illness is an opportunity for transformation.

Some suppressed material manifests quite quickly in the physical. We feel upset and come out in a rash that afternoon. We feel unspeakably angry with someone and we lose our voice next day. More deeply suppressed emotion frequently takes six months to crystalise into illness. Very often cancer develops two years after trauma or the death of someone we love.

Some people just lose the will to live when a loved one dies or after a trauma, so they open themselves to cancer. On holiday I was talking to someone who runs a cancer self-help group. She said to me that they often considered cancer to be a respectable form of suicide.

Then she told me this story about a young mother who had come to the self-help group to share her story. The young woman told them that some years ago she had been in a stressed state and she found she was pregnant. Her marriage was not good. She felt pressured by her in laws. She said to her husband. 'It's me or the baby.' Her husband and the in-laws made it clear they wanted the baby.

She later realized that it was at that moment she took a decision not to live. Soon after the little boy was born she developed cancer. The disease spread rapidly and the prognosis for her life was poor. As she hated the child and the family she didn't really care particularly.

At this point she received extensive counselling and realised that she could made different choices about her life and relationships. She realized that she could live and enjoy life. During the counselling she learnt to love the child. She claimed her power with her husband and learnt to love him too.

Her cancer gradually receded and now she was clear of it.

And at a deeper level still we bring these unreleased cellular memories from other lives to work on.

Any soul memory we are ready to work on comes up in our body for attention. Pain and disease are opportunities to grow.

If we haven't dealt with our emotions in a past life, we will bring that issue forward to re-examine. For example, if at the point of death we hold violent emotions which we can't express we will retain the memory of them in our consciousness until we give ourselves an opportunity to bring them back to awareness. When we construct our body, our consciousness will build the soul memory into the cells of the part of our body where we held the original trauma.

So if we were hanged, executed or strangled we are likely to have neck problems.

If we never expressed grief, we may have depression, asthma or the unshed tears of chronic catarrh or sinus problems.

If we were raped or sexually abused we may deaden our sexuality or have painful menstruation or be impotent.

These conditions may not occur until something happens to trigger the soul memory.

So if we felt paralysed with rage, jealousy, hurt or fear in another life, when we meet a similar situation in this one we may respond with a frozen shoulder, polio or perhaps Parkinson's disease.

Soul memories may be triggered by meeting a person whom we unconsciously recognise from another life, by a radio or television programme, by reading a book or an article about a place, event or person, by an accident or simply by being ready to look within.

Graham had been seeing me for some time. He was a very sensitive, aware and spiritual man. On this particular day, he talked about a pain in his side. The pain was right over his appendix scar and he felt bloated and uncomfortable. He couldn't immediately connect with what was causing the pain now but recalled having his appendix out when he was ten years old.

At a conscious level he couldn't remember what was

going on in the family at that time but when he closed his eyes and imagined himself back in the time just before the operation, he could feel and sense the pressure his father put him under. It was imperative he study and pass his exams. He felt squeezed and trapped. He feared failure and letting his family down. They were very powerful feelings for a child to handle and the pressure went into his weak area, his appendix.

Graham wanted to explore the source of the problem and found himself in a past life where he was the ruler of a principality. He was just and fair and everyone relied on him. On this particular night he had ridden out to a meeting and was betrayed and ambushed. He was stabbed right at the point of the appendix.

As he died he felt impotent rage and the feeling he had let his people down by letting himself be ambushed and killed. He held those feelings in his consciousness and the cellular memory of his body responded when his father triggered the same feelings within him in this life. This time his appendix ruptured.

In regression Graham expressed the rage and fury which he hadn't been able to in the other life. Then he passed over and reviewed the whole situation from a higher perspective. For the first time he became aware that murder is a contract between souls and looked at the higher reason for this choice in that life. He understood then that he had taken responsibility for the welfare of the people he ruled and so they never learnt to take responsibility for themselves. As he understood this and saw that his death was part of their learning process, he was able to meet this killers in spirit and forgive them.

The acknowledgement of his anger, the bringing to awareness of the spiritual causes of his death and the forgiveness and understanding of the whole situation, have released the repressed emotions held at his appendix point. The energy can flow in that area of his body where he previously had a blockage.

Where energy flows we are healthy.

When he opened his eyes, I asked if he could now

connect with what had caused him to have the pain and swelling now. He smiled ruefully and recognised a certain situation at work. The pain and swelling had gone by next day.

Graham only looked back into one life. Some people create the same body problems lifetime after lifetime.

I liked Hannah. She was very gentle and kind and I instinctively felt she could never hurt anyone or anything. She had many of her own past life flashes and awarenesses and had done much work on herself. She phoned for an appointment because she had to undergo a course of dental treatment. The first two sessions had proved traumatic in the extreme because she felt she couldn't breathe and had gagged and choked during the treatment. She felt there must be some deep issues involved.

She was right. When we explored, she went back to a traumatic incident in her childhood when she was nearly smothered by her very sick mother. Then she slipped into a past life in Greece where, as a young man, she was crushed in a stadium accident. She didn't feel ready to die and felt intense fear and horror as her body was trampled on.

When she left her trampled body and passed into the Light, the spirit who met her and helped her to come to terms with her horrible death was the same mother who had tried to smother her in this one. Clearly there was much between them at a soul level. Hannah moved on to an Egyptian life where she was a young boy initiate. These initiation ceremonies are very carefully prepared for and of course, failure means death. The priest who prepared the young Egyptian boy was once again the mother she was so karmically linked with.

That young boy so long ago was buried in a tomb where he had learnt to go into trance, so that he barely breathed and could survive for many hours with limited oxygen. He panicked and smothered to death. Hannah re-experienced the horror of this death and let all the feelings go. She also forgave herself for panicking and the priest for his share in the situation.

I didn't see her again for some months. When I did, she

told me there was no more problem with gagging and choking in the dentist's chair. The remainder of the treatment went forward smoothly.

Failed initiations inevitably seem to bring forward problems, probably because the sense of shame and failure are so strong. George had a blockage in his throat centre. It manifest as a stammer. Again we went back to several lives where he was trapped and did not dare to shout for help, resulting in much blocked throat energy. Then he found himself in a life as a young american indian about to take his initiation ceremony. He failed for trying to help another initiate and was cast out alone in the darkness. While he was in anguish over his failed initiation, a snake slithered over and bit him in the throat. He died, unable to call for help.

Releasing the blocked energy helped his stammer considerably but his throat is still his weak centre if he is under stress.

Many thousands of souls incarnating now have been persecuted in other lives for healing. A large proportion of them have been put to death as witches. And now these people are attracted to working in the natural therapies. Many carry deep cellular memories of burning, hanging, drowning, being buried alive or other atrocities.

Some years ago I was on a workshop. We were in the middle of a guided meditation and I had obviously gone off on my own inner journey, for the workshop leader suddenly called out to me. 'What you are seeing at this moment is the reason for your eye problems.' At that moment I was seeing myself being burnt at the stake as a witch.

That picture has stayed with me. It explains some of the reason why I am short sighted. At some level I am afraid of seeing a future where I might be burnt at the stake for my beliefs or my work. My vision has improved but I have more to explore – more opportunities for growth

Carl was a dedicated therapist, very sensitive, and working in many areas with crystals, colour, energy balancing and esoteric arts. He was also a very charming and capable man. For years he had had a neck problem. We explored his anger towards his parents but that yielded no particular information. However when we looked at the source of the problem he found himself as a witch in a female body.

He had been a wise woman, a gentle healer and had taught universal wisdom ... but the villagers didn't understand. When one of the villagers died they accused the quiet gentle recluse who worked with herbs and gentle remedies of witchcraft. They dug a pit and buried her in it up to her neck and hurled obscenities at her while she died a slow painful and frustrating death. As Carl saw himself in that situation he could feel intense pain in his neck. He felt so angry, so humiliated and so misunderstood. As he died he felt a deep unremitting anger towards those persecutors.

It wasn't until he went back into the scene and looked at the villagers' fears that he began to understand. He saw their fear based on ignorance. He became aware that their fear was a reflection of the fear that he had held as that gentle old recluse.

He began to understand and send light to the personality he had been then. As he did so, the personality who was the old recluse felt compassion for the villagers. For a split second, she felt total oneness with them. As Carl sensed her forgiving them he felt his neck pain relax.

Forgiveness releases the divine energy held in our cells and frees us to be whole and healed. This divine energy then flows like a wave through the Universe, bathing everyone in its path in Light.

It is time now for forgiveness. It is time now for Transformation.

SIXTEEN

Claiming Our Power

It is time now for women to claim their womanhood. It is also time for men to claim their manhood.

For too long women have let themselves be used and abused and given their power away. We have let it happen. The belief of women that they are powerless is held in the collective unconscious. Every time a woman claims her power or lets go of old inappropriate beliefs, she does it for all women.

Ultimately she does it for all men too, for everyone gains when balance is restored.

Where women have given power away, they have traditionally used manipulations, nagging and the withholding of love to get their revenge. These weapons of powerlessness are no longer appropriate.

And when sons are born to women who are angry with men, they are subtly punished. This means they grow up into men who feel they are somehow not quite good enough.

They may feel unloved, manipulated or simply unable ever to please women. In some families the opposite happens and boys are put onto pedestals to become the hope of the family. This is a precarious position to be in and very frightening. It is often so subtly done that no one is consciously aware of what is happening.

And these men, feeling powerless to get the love and nurturing they crave from mothers, sisters, wives and daughters, feel angry. Some have sexually used and abused women as a substitute for love. Or they have deflected their rage at their inability to be truly loved by fighting in wars or by controlling people.

These defences are no longer appropriate. They are a denial of manhood. If being a woman is a hindrance we, in turn, deny our womanhood. If we are abused or devalued as women we will not flow as a woman. When we find being a woman uncomfortable we have menstrual problems.

Gill had suffered for many years from pre-menstrual tension. It completely wrecked one week out of every month and as a very spiritual being she knew it was time to take responsibility for herself. We had worked together for several sessions on childhood confusion and abuse. At this point she saw a clairvoyant friend who told her that she had a brown smudge in her aura which was something unhealed from another life.

When she came for her next session her unconscious mind indicated that there were two past lives which were influencing her pre-menstrual tension. One was in the early twentieth century and the other in the eighteenth century.

She quickly regressed into the early twentieth century. She was in her early teens, young and innocent, living on a farm. She had a young man, whom she one day expected to marry. On this day they had had a quarrel and she felt miserable and out of sorts.

It was during the afternoon that she heard the sound of heavy boots, a sound which in this life had terrified her. A gang of five soldiers came up to the farm and demanded food. She was rude to them, partly because she was feeling miserable and partly because she was afraid they would hurt her mother. But they grabbed her and dragged her into the barn and all five of them gang-raped her. Her rage and sense of violation was enormous. With her eyes screwed up tight and her jaw clenched, she vowed, 'I'll make myself strong. No man will ever hurt me again.'

After the rape she never saw her young man again. He went to war and was killed. For the rest of that life she hated all men. Her mother looked after her and tried to help her but she just didn't want to live.

When she passed over from that life into the Light, her awareness was that if she had let the soldiers in and given them food with her heart open, they wouldn't have harmed her in any way.

After that session, she felt much better but her left shoulder and neck and left leg started hurting. They felt strangely bruised and sore and she felt sure it was connected with the work we had done and that something was coming up from a deeper level. So I took Gill back again into that life when she was gang-raped. This time she experienced that the men had held her down on the left side of her body while each in turn violated her.

She really connected with her feelings and screamed abuse and obscenities as she flailed a cushion which represented one of the men. Her left leg kicked and kicked in a way it couldn't during the actual outrage. After the release of these repressed emotions, her shoulder, neck and left leg felt completely better.

Gill was a beautifully refined lady and was somewhat appalled when she remembered the language she had used but I reminded her that she was in touch with deep atavistic anger and also that the personality of that farm girl was very different from the person she was now!

It was also during this second session that she brought to awareness the fact that one of the men who raped her was Andrew, her partner in this life.

Interestingly, Andrew's father had, during the First World War shot some men in a barn for raping a woman. Andrew had had a recurring dream all his life of being shot by his father. The shooting occurred sixteen years before Andrew was born.

It helped Gill to see many things differently in her relationship with Andrew. She started to claim her power and after a few weeks she ended the relationship and never regretted it. It felt like a karmic completion.

Gill had recognised that her young man in that life was a former boyfriend in this. He had independently done a past life regression some years before where he had quarrelled with his girl friend and gone off to war. He had died in a trench with a bayonet in his back. When Gill next saw her clairvoyant friend, she was told that the brown patch in her aura had almost completely disappeared.

Her pre-menstrual tension had become much less of a problem but she wanted to explore the eighteenth century life too. This, it transpired, had been a life in France. She and her twin brother, Pierre, lived in a large château, in isolation except for servants. She and Pierre relied exclusively on each other and did everything together. When they were thirteen, he had to go away to war. The pain in her solar plexus was excruciating. And she was angry about being a woman, angry about periods which stopped her going to battle with her brother. She was also very afraid.

Pierre died in battle and never returned. She was expected to be strong. She never showed her grief or fear and the rest of her life passed in an aching grieving, emptiness.

As Gill relived the old experience she released the deep tears she had held back then. When she went through her death to the other side, she found that her twin, Pierre, was there to greet her. She was transformed with joy and when he told her that all the grieving was unnecessary and it was time to accept her womanhood, she knew he was right.

If we feel shame or guilt, we will unconsciously punish ourselves. Starvation is self-inflicted punishment in an effort to avoid womanhood. Many anorexics have past life histories of abuse.

Sophie couldn't cope with growing up. The thought of having a boyfriend made her feel panicky. She didn't know how to cope, so she starved herself until her periods stopped. Her mother had never really accepted her femininity or sexuality, so Sophie had no role model for comfortable womanhood. Her father was irritable, authoritarian and distant, so he was not comfortable as a man.

A little girl's father is the first man to show her that she is acceptable as a woman. If he can convey to her that she is O.K. as a girl, she can grow up to feel safe with men. If he feels uncomfortable or powerless in his manhood, he cannot validate her as a girl.

So Sophie's father couldn't help Sophie to feel acceptable or that it was safe to grow up to be a woman and have a loving relationship with a man. And, as an embryonic woman, she took in learnings that it was dangerous to be a woman. She didn't dare grow up.

As we explored her inner world, she started to adjust her beliefs about herself. She became more comfortable and relaxed with her parents. But she did not feel safe enough to let her periods start.

At this point in our work together she spontaneously regressed into another life where she had been raped and murdered as a teenager. Then she found a life where she had died in childbirth when she was barely fifteen. In a third session she found herself in service as a young girl and was sexually abused by her master. She had a child by him and was turned out into the streets where she had to beg. The baby died.

Small wonder she was afraid to be a woman. At an unconscious level she believed that to grow into womanhood meant abuse, loss and death. And, like so many abused women, she unconsciously believed that somehow she was to blame for all the abuse perpetrated on her.

She certainly attracted the abuse. She was not to blame for it. Any shame belongs to the perpetrator not the victim. However, if we feel guilty about something, other people will pick up our guilt and feed it back to us by unconsciously blaming us. They will therefore punish us in some way and we will let them.

Now Sophie could let it all go. She no longer let other people punish her by subtly putting her down or disempowering her.She no longer needed to punish herself by starving herself. Her periods started again after the third regression.

I took her then to experience several lives where she had been happily married and had had children and had safely enjoyed being a woman. Gradually she started to put on weight.

There are still conflicts within her psyche to be resolved. However, she is an old soul who is resolutely working to claim her power to be an open, loving, lovable woman. When she totally accepts her womanhood she will be able to empower men.

The room went ice cold when Malcolm walked in for his first appointment. I sensed there was going to be heavy work.

His presenting problem was complete deadness in his hands and sometimes his feet. He had had every sort of medical check but nothing showed. We also discussed his feelings towards women. He was so angry towards them. At least he had deep abiding anger towards his mother and this he deflected onto women in general. Hating and mistrusting women as he did, he did not feel comfortable as a man.

He was certain that the answers to his problems lay in experiences before this life, as nothing had shown up in any other therapy he had done.

He contacted very little during that first session but enough to keep him intrigued and determined to come back. When eventually he was able to connect with his far memories, he found lifetime after lifetime where he felt unloved and rejected by women.

In one his mother died when he was a child. In another he was abandoned. In another his nurse abused him. There was no one to show him the feminine attributes of loving, caring and nurturing. And in each case he had to bury the feelings. When we don't feel our feelings we don't feel other people's either. In each of those lives he became very cruel in his efforts to deny his hurting inner child.

In one life of barbarous fighting, his reputation for cruelty was such that when he was captured, the enemy chopped off his hands as trophies.

In another life his hands were chopped off for stealing. In a third he was taken prisoner and cruelly tied by his hands and feet until they went dead.

In each lifetime he had tried to bury his pain towards women by becoming outwardly brave and macho. He raped and pillaged to get revenge, but nothing healed the hurt.

In the work that we did he began to get sensation back in his extremities. He felt it was even more important that he started to accept his hurting child. He began to accept his feminine side which allowed him to nurture and be nurtured as he had not experienced for lifetimes.

This in turn allowed him to feel more safe and comfortable as a man. As he claimed his manhood, he started to relate to women.

When a man claims his manhood he can honour women.
When a woman claims her womanhood she can honour men.
Then we have peace on Earth.

It is time for each of us to learn to love ourselves. It is time now for each of us to empower ourself as a man or woman, so that this transformation can take place now.

SEVENTEEN

Obsessions

Any obsessive, compulsive or addictive behaviour is a way of keeping unacceptable feelings at bay.

By repeating a ritual, whether it is a repetitive thought or action, we are taking our minds off the underlying deep need and keeping ourselves safe.

Most of us try to protect ourselves from feelings of underlying despair, panic, aloneness, unworthiness or the meaninglessness of life by some sort of ritual behaviour.

Some of us do it by addictive drinking, eating, smoking, drug taking. Others use compulsive behaviour, such as gambling, talking, blaming, overspending, sex, driving too fast. We can be obsessed with jealousy, anger, guilt or with a person. And we may need help and strength to overcome the problem.

Being a workaholic is considered to be socially acceptable but being an alcoholic or a bulimic is not. All are destructive and serve to defend the vulnerable inner personalities from feeling pain. These defences also prevent us from growing into balanced people, and we need to let them go.

Most people with addictions and compulsions, even obsessions, are sustained in their problem by those around them.

An alcoholic often has a partner who colludes by covering up for the drinker, at the same time constantly reinforcing his bad feelings about himself by telling him he is bad. The colluder always feels angry and out of control. They are often dependent on the alcoholic remaining addicted to keep them feeling they are needed. And while they focus their attention externally on their partner, they don't have to look at their own feelings and behaviour.

The workaholic is usually driven by the expectations of those near him. Most are still secretly trying to get the approval of their parents, even where the parents are long since dead. The wife of one big businessman, who is extremely successful and a total workaholic, told me that he never tells his parents of his promotions or successes. He thinks they wouldn't be interested. The father of another workaholic told me that his son was so pleased to get a first at Cambridge. 'My son said he only wanted it for me.' That grown-up son is still working obsessionally to please his father.

Rageoholics, those addicted to angry feelings, are sustained by the fear their families and others have of them. They use rage to cover up their feelings of powerlessness. Other people's fear of them feeds them and gives them a vicarious feeling of power. Inevitably, their constant rage means that those closest to them don't trust them. Their rage serves to keep them separate. This constantly reinforces the frightened, unloved feeling they hold in the core of their being.

When we focus on sex, spending, driving fast cars or gambling we don't have to feel the pain of reality as we perceive it. When we become obsessed by something we can become possessed by our own negative thought forms.

I never underestimate the power of obsessional thoughts, for I had a very nasty experience many years ago soon after I got divorced.

I realised later just how angry I had been for a very long time at men and my ex husband in particular. At that time I tried to be 'nice'. I didn't know how to deal with the rage. I simply had no understanding or skills about claiming power and dissolving anger. So I suppressed it. The suppressed angry thoughts created a huge dark energy cloud in the shape of a man. When I brooded on my anger one night, I energised this huge negative thought form.

That night I was in bed, half asleep and half awake. To

my horror I watched the shadow of an enormous man, about nine feet tall, climb through the window and lumber towards me. In that instant I felt my young son get into bed beside me to protect me. I could actually touch and feel his physical presence. In reality he was in boarding school many miles away. Then I escaped out of my body into the bathroom.

Later, when I returned to my body and woke up fully, I felt considerably shaken by the incident. I realised that what I had experienced was my own negative energy towards men formed into the shape of a huge man, coming to attack me. And my son had clearly felt the danger at a soul level and astrally projected to my side to protect me. I was astonished that I could feel his physical body.

Then I closed my eyes and visualized the negative thought cloud and started to dissolve it with golden light. At the same time, on a practical level I started to look at and find ways to deal with my anger, and to make my life more fun and more balanced.

I can see now how the hate, anger, hurt and bitterness I held at that time were being stored in my lower chakras. When I started to see the Light, to meditate, to try to raise my vibrations, the heavy vibrations held in my lower chakras could no longer be contained. They then had to be dealt with.

Imagine a swing. On the forward movement we swing into the sunlight. The backswing takes us into the shadow of a tree. As we grow we go through the same process. If we aim to swing higher into the Light we must at the same time swing higher into the dark or negative. We can't reach one without experiencing the other. When we aim to the Light we have to accept our shadow. If our aura is weak, wispy and grey, we are open to all negative thoughts around us.

A strong aura is as protective as a souwester and is imperme-able to negativity.

Clearly when in the grip of an obsessional emotion we need to strengthen our aura.

To strengthen our aura we need to

> Have fun and laugh a lot
> Do lots of exercise and dance
> Listen to inspirational music and speakers
> Read inspiring books
> Do exciting and interesting things. Get out of the rut.
> Meet new people
> Think happy and positive thoughts.

If we have a desperate need to be loved we sometimes become obsessional about a person who appears to fulfil our needs. Inge hadn't had a fulfilling relationship for many years, if ever. But she had done a lot of personal growth work and was beginning to feel really comfortable with herself. She had built up her interests and had lots of friends of both sexes.

And then, pow, she met Keith. Inge fell with a bang. From that first meeting she could think of nothing else. He was in her mind all the time. Keith became a total obsession.

Luckily Inge was normally a very balanced and sensible lady. After their next couple of meetings when the obsession hadn't abated, she realized that there must be unfinished business from another life between them. She called a friend who was a therapist and asked him to help her explore any past relationship. This is the story she told me.

I found that Keith had been my husband in another life. It was a tribal life where men had several wives. I was very young and was his third wife. But we loved each other very much. He was very caring and looked after me. The village wise person told me that I would bear him five sons. We had three fine sons and I was pregnant with the fourth child. I was very happy and fulfilled.

Then they brought me news that he had been bitten by a snake and died. I couldn't believe it. I was in shock. The wise man had told me I would bear five sons. Something was wrong. As it turned out I had twin sons born after his death. But I never got over it.

As so often happens, when something is unfinished in another life we bring it forward to complete. When Inge met Keith, the memory of and longing for that beautiful relationship they had once enjoyed took over completely.

As soon as Inge had the awareness of the past life, the obsession went totally. They were able to become friends. And a few weeks after that she was able to realise that they had very little in common in this life. It was his remembered qualities that she had been looking for. She was able to write to him quite calmly and tell him she no longer wanted to see him.

Sometimes past life exploration reveals that we have undertaken to clear a family miasm. Karen had an obsession with her boyfriend, Malcolm. Now that he had ended the relationship she was beside herself with grief. Nothing would console her and the doctor put her on tranquillisers because she couldn't work.

We worked for several sessions to help her to understand her patterns and to feel better. Then she slipped into a past life exploration to gain greater awareness.

She found herself in a life where she obsessively loved her husband to the exclusion of her five children, two boys and three girls. She recognised her husband then as Malcolm. When he died in that life she was inconsolable. Her children had scattered and didn't want to know her. She died eventually of total devastation and loneliness.

Karen was so startled with the impact of this session and the vividness of the pictures that she phoned her mother to tell her about it. Her mother too was startled. She said, 'You are describing in detail you great-grandmother's story. She neglected her children, two boys and three girls and was obsessed with her husband. She too finally died of a broken heart after years of isolation and loneliness. Karen realised that she had undertaken to clear something for the whole family.

The Earth plane can be beautiful and joy-filled when we are ready to raise our vibrations to perceive it. We can lift the lid off the seething cauldron of negativity within and make dramatic awarenesses and changes.

The joy of working with Divine Energy is that amazing things happen all the time.

Vivienne had been an occasional client of mine for years, coming for a few sessions whenever she was in crisis. She worried about everything. If she had a cold, she expected it to become pneumonia. She couldn't sleep at night thinking she had cancer. A tiny spot was evidence of a tumour. Every pain she was convinced was terminal.

As well as obsessional fear about her health, she was terrified of everything. She expected her family to die. She constantly anticipated everything going wrong. She was addicted to worry.

I was working with her on a childhood issue. Then I had the impression I must take her back through birth into the corridor before life. She found herself in a corridor of doors and I asked her to open whichever door was appropriate to find the information she needed to help her with her life. She opened a door and it was blinding Light ahead. I asked how she felt and she said it was worrying! She told me a wise person was with her helping her to hold the Light in her heart and keep it there.

Then she kept repeating. 'I'm trying to get rid of the fear so I can walk into the Light and accept it . . . oh I can't do it. The fears are holding onto me.'

I kept urging her to leap into the Light but she kept crying that she couldn't do it.

'Yes, you *can*,' I almost shouted.

At that, she leapt. Her body jerked. She gasped. Tears poured down her cheeks. She cried out, 'It's beautiful. A beautiful place.'

She wanted to stay and I left her in bliss for a time. Then I asked her to bring the Light back into her life. She glowed. She radiated. And she kept repeating, 'It was the Earth. It was the Earth.'

She told me her experience was here, right now on Earth but all golden . . . a different perception of everything. 'I believe it but it's unbelievable,' she said. 'Life is different from what I thought it was. Everything is different.'

That experience transformed Vivienne's life. Nothing

ever was the same again. I felt privileged to share her experience.

The joy of working with Divine Energy is that amazing things happen all the time.

EIGHTEEN

Writing Our Drama

When we listen to someone talking about himself, he will soon reveal his life position statements. These are the beliefs he holds about life.

Whatever beliefs we hold we keep repeating in our conversations, like an affirmation, and we write them into the script of our life. We all write our own life story based on these beliefs. Some beliefs serve us badly and we continually put in acts that are unhappy or violent or sordid.

It is quite fascinating to listen to people talking and pick out the story themes.

Many people make betrayal statements and we can be sure the drama they are choosing to write will include being let down in their work environment or in relationships. Invariably these script writers are paranoid.

> You can't trust anyone.
> You get stabbed in the back.
> I wouldn't trust him as far as I could throw him.
> They always let you down.
> You can't rely on men/women.
> You've got to watch them like hawks.

Many of us feel safe in our little world of home and work and friends but have a great fear of 'out there'. These scripts include

> It's a hard life

> It's a big bad world
> There's no place like home.

Very often something awful will have happened to them in an old story, in another life, when they ventured outside their village.

Similarly, if we have had lives where we failed and perhaps died feeling disappointed in ourselves, we continue to write failure scripts. We may even set ourselves an impossible task, thus guaranteeing failure. We will use expressions like.

> I'm not good enough.
> It's hopeless.
> It's no use trying.
> I'm a failure.
> What's the use.
> I'll never do it.

If we let someone down or perhaps we perceive we let the side down, we hear ourselves saying,

> I don't deserve.
> It's my fault.
> I always get it wrong.

We may go to the other extreme and become driving, striving script writers, determined to try harder and getting knotted with tension.

> I've got to try harder.
> No-one's going to stop me.
> I'll do it or die in the attempt.

Poverty writers say

> It's hard to make ends meet.
> There's never enough.
> Save for a rainy day.

And of course when we believe in danger we affirm

> Better safe than sorry.
> It's a jungle out there.

It takes the same amount of energy to make sure we build positive life statements into our scripts and watch how the story of our life, act by act, begins to run smoothly, happily and successfully.

Successful people constantly say,

> I always succeed in the end.
> I can do it.
> Where there's a will there's a way.
> I always fall on my feet.

Happy people look for the silver lining.

> I'm lucky
> There's good in everybody.
> There are lots of nice people around.
> It's great to have good friends.
> Friends are always there when you need them.
> God's on my side.

Prosperous people write into their life

> There's plenty to go round.
> There's more where that came from.

Pauline came to see me because of her relationship problems. She was pretty and rounded and feminine, with soft wavy hair. As I listened to her talking about her family and work, I became aware that the expressions she was using were almost bizarre in the context. Her conversation was laced with military terms.

> You get no quarter.
> There's no second chance.
> They'll get you if you're not careful.
> You've got to be on your guard.

Intrigued, I asked her if her family had military connections but she said there were none. When she closed her eyes to look for the source of her problems I fed these military terms back to her and she at once found herself in a male body, as a soldier in battle. She described the old battle scenes of jungle warfare with horror on her face.

As a young soldier he had been terrified. The enemy were orientals and attack came suddenly and unexpectedly. The soldiers had to be alert and on guard every moment and if anyone was captured the consequences were horrific.

In that life the young soldier became brutalised and battle scarred and when he went home to marry the fiancée he'd left behind, he couldn't leave the old battle beliefs behind and the relationship couldn't work, despite the fact that he loved her deeply. In despair he re-enlisted and deliberately put himself into a dangerous position where he would be killed.

And, so that she could take another look at these issues, Pauline wrote the soldier script into this life.

As all these awarenesses surfaced, Pauline began to open her heart and transform. The following week she reported that several people had remarked how different she was. And her boyfriend, who had said he didn't want to see her again and refused to meet her, had been to see her and they had started communicating again.

Sometimes we seem determined to hold onto our old scripts. They are still serving a need and we have to continue acting out the consequences.

One man I know was a poor communicator. This let him down at work and caused endless misunderstandings. On one level he wanted to change this and be able to communicate warmly and clearly. He talked to me in some depth about the problem.

He kept telling me how awful he was on the phone. He hated the phone. He called it the ten ton monster. He referred to it as the barrier between himself and his clients, to be overcome.

I pointed out to him how he was re-affirming to himself constantly his life scripts. After all, the phone could be considered as a bridge between himself and his clients. I said perhaps it would help to make a positive affirmation before he spoke on the phone.

I suggested:

I speak on the phone
In a warm and friendly tone.

He looked me firmly in the eye and said, 'Don't be silly. I've told you. I'm hopeless on the phone.'

He really wants to learn his lesson the hard way.

Many people have scripts about not being understood. This can be difficult to change because if we feel no one understands us then we are constantly trying to explain ourselves. And however hard the others try to understand, however much they listen, because of our belief, we feel they don't understand.

Looking at the old stories can help in the changing of this belief. As I listened to Susannah, there were two constantly re-iterated phrases – 'I've had enough' and 'They don't understand.'

Her marriage had been destroyed because she constantly felt put upon and unsupported. 'I kept telling him I've had enough' , she repeated. She was very confused about her role as wife and mother. Her frustration was enormous and destructive. She expected her husband to understand her when she didn't understand herself.

Then she started to talk about how withdrawn and quiet her son had become. She found him very annoying. His untidy bedroom annoyed her. So did his music practice. I keep saying to him, 'I've had enough,' she said, 'but he doesn't understand and I can't get anything out of him'.

I helped her to open her heart centre and to see what was really going on for the little boy. She realised then how terrified he was of her leaving him. She became aware that her expression of 'I've had enough' and the vibrations of frustration that she gave off put the child into paralytic terror and he survived in the only way he knew how – by becoming silent and withdrawn and hoping to escape notice. She also became aware of the enormity of her own needs for love and nurturing and that her attitudes were stopping her from ever getting them met.

As these awarenesses came to her, I fed the phrases, 'I've

had enough', and 'No one understands' to her and asked
her to bring up a memory of the source of these beliefs.

She saw herself in another life. Her son in this life was
her husband then. 'I feel angry and frustrated. I can't get
him to do what I want. I keep saying to him, 'You don't
understand,' but he doesn't know what to do. I keep telling
him, 'I've had enough,' but he doesn't change. We keep
quarrelling because he doesn't understand what I want.
He's becoming quieter and quieter and more withdrawn.
It's as if there is a great wall between us'.

Then she moved to the point where her husband died
and gave a heartrending sob. 'He's died. The wall's gone.
He loves me. He loved me all the time. I never realized how
much he loved me. He was frightened I'd leave him.'

She saw with vivid clarity that her frustration and anger
had pushed him behind a wall. She saw that she had done
the same to her husband in this life and that she was
repeating the pattern with the man who was her husband
and was now her child.

It was a sobering moment of self-responsibility. She
softened and it was as if a lump lifted from her heart. The
next time I saw her, she said that her son was coming out of
his shell and everything seemed much brighter.

I had known Geraldine slightly for some time when she
came to see me. She came from a genteel, upper middle
class background. Physically she was attractive and elfin-
like in her movements. I knew that she was very creative
and artistic and obviously very sensitive and intuitive.

She told me that she lacked confidence with people and
when she was in company she often felt a misfit. When she
didn't feel accepted by people, she felt tension in her throat
and wanted to cry. As a small child her family lived in
America, where she had felt happy and comfortable. It
wasn't until the age of six, when they moved to England,
that the misfit feelings started. At school she felt different
because of her accent. She didn't belong. After two terms,
the family moved house and she tried to settle into another
school but she had the same feeling of not belonging.

In an earlier session we had looked at these six year old

feelings and she felt we had peeled a layer off the onion. Now I asked her to focus on the throat tension and on the familiar thoughts, 'I'm a misfit. I'm different. No one wants me.'

Geraldine experienced her throat tightening and she felt she was being dragged along by a rope round her neck. She saw herself as a man, a half caste. His mother was black and he was accepted in the black community. But he was bright and forthright and wanted to be accepted by the white community. Because of his attitude the white community feared him.

Suddenly Geraldine's body went rigid and dead with helplessness as she relived the torment of that former life. 'They're hanging me . . . two white men . . . but I didn't do it. I'm innocent.' He couldn't shout or do anything because the rope was choking him.

He realized he'd been set up – accused of stealing because they wanted him out of the way. The white women had jeered at him as he was dragged away to be hanged.

The body of the woman in the chair choked and gagged as she re-experienced the trauma still alive in her unconscious. Then, as that young man in the old story, he felt the release into death. As he died he realized that his deep resentment about being half caste and not accepted, caused him to be aggressive and outspoken. He became aware of just how entrenched the white people's fear was of him.

Now from a higher level of understanding, he imagined himself back in that life. This time he watched himself living his life without bitterness or resentment. Filled with self worth and confidence he was no threat to anyone and experienced himself being accepted by both sides as he was.

When Geraldine opened her eyes she was amazed at the awareness that she had just had. She immediately made more connections and told me that when she started at her first school in England, there was one black girl in the school and they became friends. This little black child helped her enormously to feel settled. Then when she moved to her next school, she became friendly with a half caste child and they became firm friends.

She said that all her life most of her close friends had been black. More and more awarenesses flooded in for her. At that time a half black cousin was living with her family.

It seems she and her whole family were learning lessons in acceptance on many levels.

After the awarenesses she had had during her regression, Geraldine felt much more composed and comfortable in herself. Her tension eased and she started to write a new script for her life, filled with acceptance and confidence.

NINETEEN

Relationships

We have all experienced traumas and difficult relationships in our past lives. It is not what actually occurs that registers in our unconscious and causes later problems but our attitudes and what we held in our thoughts at that time.

If we are killed by someone we may, although it is unlikely, feel a sense of total understanding and forgiveness for that person. In that case it isn't a trauma for us, and because it hasn't recorded in our personal records, we don't re-create or re-attract those same conditions.

This is what Jesus did on the cross. Instead of recording rage and hatred for his persecutors, he forgave them. So no karma was created. Grace released all.

However, if we felt hatred and a desire for revenge on our persecutors, *that* registers within us. And the force of suppressed hatred and desire for revenge we hold down inside us is the exact force that we need to release. In subsequent lives we will subconsciously play the record, 'I hate you. I want revenge', with that same energy force. With this unconscious programme, we will make enemies.

If we hold a vengeful predator in our head we will be cruel. The hate and vengeance may become generalized or it may be triggered when we meet our original persecutor.

So what is done to us we will do back to the same people or others.

The two polarities are always with us. We see-saw between being murderer and murdered, perpetrator and victim, betrayer and betrayed. And this swinging from one side to the other has been going on for far too long in terms of the evolution of the planet. We are being called on to look at these long standing negative patterns and stop them, so that we can evolve by raising our consciousness to higher levels.

As part of this raising of consciousness we are feeling the energy of the Aquarian age. This Aquarian energy is shaking people up and raising their vibrations. And as the energy is beginning to lift, more and more people are having access to their past lives.

When we see the total picture it is so much easier to feel differently about everything. Then we sit in the middle of the see-saw and accept and forgive both sides. We no longer sit on one side or the other. At that point we have total conscious awareness.

Pure conscious awareness is a point of Grace. We have 'got' that lesson. We never have to do it again and we have taken steps forward on our journey to the Light.

This is how Queenie brought a whole pattern to conscious awareness and with humility and love dissolved a tangled ball of karma. Queenie was a natural medium. She was also very caring and funny and immensely likeable.

However she was fat, very fat and desperately conscious of it. She dealt with the outside world by presenting a joky, it's O.K. to make fun of me, facade. This disguised from the world the hurt inside. Naturally, when people did make fun of her, she seethed with anger. Her impulse was to sizzle them with sarcasm but she joked and swallowed down the rage with sweets and chocolate.

She felt an overpowering sense of being trapped, she told me – trapped in her marriage, trapped by her children, trapped by fate. In her twenties her mother had had an affair with a married man and become pregnant with Queenie. Her father chose to stay with his wife and family, so he was never there for her in this lifetime.

Queenie's mother felt angry, bitter and betrayed. She scarcely had time for herself, let alone a daughter. So Queenie felt unwanted. She also felt unacknowledged by her father, which was a deep resentment inside her.

So the old records she had brought with her into this life

were, 'I'm trapped', 'No-one is there for me', 'I'm unacknowledged' and these tapes, playing constantly in her mind, were causing problems in her marriage and with her family.

When she had told me her story, I helped her open her heart centre and she lit up like a flame. All the memories of who she really was, a being of Light and Love, all the knowing of the Spiritual Laws, all the understanding that we are spirit manifest in matter for this incarnation, were there. She only needed to be reminded.

We worked over the next few weeks to heal her relationship with herself – and therefore with her family.

Queenie had her set backs, her put-downs where she seethed with rage and old wounds festered and were cleaned out. Each time she opened her heart and re-connected with the Truth of who she was and healed something.

Because she was moving to another part of the country I knew there were only two more sessions and simply asked for guidance to use these sessions for the highest good. For the first of these two sessions she arrived complaining of shooting pains at the top of her right arm and a stiff neck. She could hardly move her arm and the pains were like knives being thrust into her. She'd had these pains once before when her second child was born. I asked her to go into the pain and see what was happening and she immediately saw herself as a man surrounded by warriors with spears.

'I'm in the middle. They are all round me. They are spearing me in my arm. Oh the pain! I fear I'll die. . . . I'm trapped. I'm trapped.'

Her feeling as she died was one of violent rage. We worked on releasing the anger. Then she looked down at the scene from a higher perspective, seeing the whole picture. Now she became aware of the fear that the warriors had. She could sense their background and beliefs and she could feel a surge of compassion and forgiveness.

That life floated away and she slipped into the feelings of her child being born. 'I'm on the table. I'm trapped. Nigel should be here. Where is he?'

She was angry with her husband, Nigel for not being there for her. In fact the nurse hadn't let him know as she had promised to do, that Queenie was giving birth.

On one level she knew that it wasn't her husband's fault but she was angry with her father for not being there for her all her life and quite naturally – we all do it – she transferred the anger onto her husband regardless of the facts.

Many a person has paid heavily for the anger their partner holds towards a parent.

At this moment she recognised that at her baby's birth she had transmitted her belief that there was no one there for her so powerfully that she had physically created her aloneness. She took responsibility for creating what happened. With her heart open, she got the lesson and forgave her husband, her face flushing with a kind of radiance. Then she found herself in a monastery. She shivered. This was a dark life indeed.

'I'm born deformed . . . my right arm is cut off . . . I can't get out of here. I'm locked in . . . in a cell . . . made to be a monk.' She slipped into the past tense as she disassociated from the pain. 'Nothing I could do . . . I was there from birth.'

Her energy returned with a rush and she says, 'I hate them. My arm's bad. It hurts.' She speaks to her jailer. 'Let me go. Let me go.'

Lapsing into the past tense again as helplessness overcame her, 'It wasn't my fault.' Then she went on with a gasp. 'The man is my father.' She sounded surprised and horrified. Her father was her jailer.

Her father in that life was her jailer. I directed her to see if she recognised him and she saw he was her grandfather in this life.

'He won't acknowledge me. He can't. He's a monk and powerful in the hierarchy.'

She started using her right arm in a frenzy of blows towards this man. 'I want to push him away. I detest him. I detest him. He killed my mother.'

She went back to her birth in that life and told me that her mother knew she had to die and described her mother's horror at giving birth to a deformed child.

She found it difficult to forgive her father but at last she said she thought she had done so. At least she felt better disposed towards him. Then she found herself in her death bed scene. She experienced herself dying slowly and crying out, 'I don't want to die. I didn't have enough time.'

Later when we examined her statement, 'I didn't have enough time', and the anguish with which it was spoken, she realized that she had had time but no motivation. She also realised that she did the same thing in this life. With that awareness she took some real decision about what she intended to do in this life.

She visualised her father, a senior monk, acknowledging her as his son in front of all the monastery. That helped enormously.

When we visualise a change in the past we create new pictures in the microfilm of our stored lives and this changes things positively in our lives. Even doing something so seemingly facile as saying boo to the person who terrorised us and then laughing, shifts and lightens an energy within us.

By the end of the session Queenie's arm no longer hurt and her neck felt freer. She left at the end of the session positively flowing, feeling she had cleared something important.

When she returned the following week for her last session she said her arm was better. She had just had one or two twinges. Now she had back pains and reported that every night she had dreams about the life where she had been speared by warriors and also the life as a trapped monk. She felt she had totally cleared the warrior life but had great difficulty forgiving the monk's father.

This time when she found herself back in the life as a monk, she saw herself like a caged animal and felt resentment as a tight ball in her stomach.

She had worked on methods of dealing with her anger in situations in her current life. Now she put these methods into practice in healing her past life anger, in order to reclaim her strength and empowerment.

She closed her eyes and I took her back into the scene as that hapless monk. Calmly she examined her feelings as the trapped imprisoned unacknowledged deformed monk. When he had total clarity around the underlying causes of these feelings, he visualised his father coming into his scene and asked him to listen. He explained carefully how he felt – without blaming or judging him. To his surprise his father listened and was calm. He exclaimed, 'He's accepting . . . and my stomach is better. I see love in his eyes and he's freeing me. I feel love from him. I feel love.'

Queenie felt a rush of energy inside her and said, 'I feel free from that karma . . . I know I'm totally free. It's wonderful.'

I instructed her then to go to the previous life, which caused her to choose a life where she was trapped. I knew there must be a polarity life somewhere.

Queenie found herself in a corridor pacing up and down. 'I'm a woman and I'm guarding someone. I feel the keys against my leg. I'm governor of someone . . . one person . . . a girl. She's by the window. Oh she *hates* me. I'm cruel . . . mentally cruel. I taunt her. She's pregnant.' She paused and said in a different voice. 'She's my Mum in this life.'

She continued with the story. 'She escapes because of my carelessness. I'm put out on the streets . . . Oh God I was heartless. No affection. I'm a virgin. I pride myself on being so upright. I judged people . . . I'm lonely on the streets. I survived but didn't learn.'

I asked her to go to her childhood that she had in that life to understand what happened to turn her into a cruel, heartless, lonely woman. Queenie cried out as she saw the scene. 'Oh my mother and father both beat me. My back is scarred. I want vengeance on everyone. My father's made me afraid of men. They're brutes.'

I suggested she let her adult self go in and talk to that scarred, beaten, vengeful little girl. She did this and gave the child healing for her back and helped that split off part of her psyche to be healed and feel loved and safe.

When she felt happier and more understanding about

herself and why she behaved as she did, we brought in the pregnant girl to whom she acted as jailer and to whom she was so cruel. She explained to the girl what had happened to her in childhood and told her how desperately sorry she was.

'Oh,' Queenie breathed, 'She's opening her arms to me. She forgives me.'

Her heart felt warm and open. Now she could see the faces of her parents in that life. She didn't recognise them from this one. And now she could forgive them totally.

Queenie opened her eyes. Her back felt better and she felt truly peaceful. She had vividly experienced being the trapper and trapped, the cruel one and the victim. From a point of equilibrium she had accepted and re-integrated those aspects of herself, so she never has to act them out again in this life or another.

TWENTY

Emotions

At the Spiritual Level everything is perfect and in Divine Right order. This is a high vibratory level where we plan all things for the growth of our souls. At this level nothing can happen to us but that we agree to it.

However, actually living our lives on earth, we have to deal with emotions. These are a heavier vibration and if we don't clear them they sit within us like a time bomb waiting to explode or they hang around us like a cloak blocking us from the Light. If we don't release our emotions they will eventually crystalize into even denser, heavier vibrations and manifest as illness or dis-ease. The physical body has the densest vibration of all.

Emotions are released psychically and physically through the fluid systems of the body. They are passed out in urine, released in sweat and tears. Blood flows to cleanse a wound. Saliva flows to break down food as do digestive juices. Wax flows in the ears.

Emotions can also be dissolved by understanding and acceptance. The heavy energy is then transmuted. But they do need to be acknowledged.

At the highest spiritual level grief on bereavement is pure selfishness. The Divine Plan is a perfect working out of lessons for our soul. We are grieving for our own selfish loss.

Planet Earth is often referred to as the prison ship because we are all imprisoned in heavy vibrations. Just imagine if you were serving a term in prison and you grew to love someone in that prison. If that person were set free it would clearly be selfish to want to keep that person in jail with you. It would be natural to grieve that you are left behind in prison but you would be happy that your loved one has his or her freedom. Death is the same. It is leaving Earth prison for the freedom of Light. So at the spiritual level we rejoice for the person passing over.

However, at the emotional level, it is very different. We feel. We mourn. We grieve. If we don't acknowledge and release our grief, we create enormous problems for ourselves.

Research shows that fifty percent of children, if they aren't allowed to grieve for the loss of a parent, never get over it. They may never form wholesome relationships. Many people develop cancer two years after the death of a loved one. So, not dealing with grief causes emotional and physical problems.

Unexpressed grief can be brought through to be dealt with from other lifetimes. Ken had been slightly depressed all his life. Tears were always just below the surface and had been so for as long as he could remember. Conventional therapy had helped somewhat to strengthen and empower him but he still felt the constant lump of sadness in his throat and a feeling of guilt all the time. For years he went through agony trying to maintain a controlled front at work.

It wasn't until we looked for a source before this life that he found himself as a child living in a native village. The village was raided and he escaped.

As the only survivor of the massacre, he wandered alone for some time and was eventually taken in by another tribe. Even though he was accepted into the tribe, he always felt the grief and loss – but he couldn't show it in case he was rejected by the new tribe.

As these memories came up he sobbed – deep sobs. He went home and cried, real releasing healing tears for two days – and it was after that that he started to feel much better. The under-the-surface tears disappeared.

Of course, when we experience grief and sorrow, it can help enormously to be aware of the Spiritual Truths, in other words to recognise the overall Plan. In the same way, if we have to go through a dark tunnel, it helps if we can see the Light at the end of the tunnel.

But if we go straight to the spiritual, avoiding the darkness of the tunnel of grief, we deny the emotional and like any form of suppression, we sustain the unacknowledged energy within us.

Linda was very aware of the spiritual. She knew the Divine Plan was perfect. She nursed her husband, Robert, through cancer after a very short but loving marriage. When I asked if I could include this story, she wanted me to use their real names, as a tribute to Robert and his life.

She told me that she and Robert had made this short contract at a soul level before they incarnated. As Robert's cancer spread and he became weaker she asked me to uncord her from him because she wanted to make absolutely sure she was not unintentionally holding him in Earth prison if he was ready to die.

I discuss cording in some detail in *Light Up Your Life*, but briefly, when we send thoughts to someone else, these thoughts create cords which attach to the other person. Through these cords we emotionally pull and manipulate each other. We also exchange energy through them. Just like someone else's blood, someone else's energy may not be right for us. And it is important we each learn to live off our own energy.

The releasing exercise involves visualising ourselves sitting in one circle and the person we are releasing from sitting in another. Then we visualise a light going round the two circles in a figure of eight. The purpose of this is to tell the unconscious mind to prepare to release the other person and to draw our own energy back to us and to return their energy to them.

Once I was uncording a client from her mother. They had exchanged so much energy, they were acting as each other. As the client was doing the figure of eight, I was shown a huge magnet and was instructed to invite the client to hold this magnet in front of her solar plexus. The magnet was specifically energised for the client's own vibration. As she did so she could feel a powerful flow in her solar plexus as her own energy was drawn back into her from her mother. She then visualised a magnet being held by her mother. This magnet was energised for her mother's energy only. She felt an even more powerful flow as the alien energy left her body.

I have since used this magnet in uncordings when prompted to do so. After this I ask my client to visualise any cords running from them to the other person. These are then cut and gently pulled from the body and burnt. The wounds are healed in an appropriate way.

I took Linda through this process and then asked her to visualise the cords. She was very surprised at what she saw. She found she was holding onto her husband at an emotional level. At a soul level she had let him go. At an emotional level she desperately wanted him to stay with her. She could feel a gaping hole of emptiness inside her. This she filled with golden light. Then she released the emotional bonds and set her beloved husband free. He died a few days later. She was able to sit by him. She found this a great comfort as she felt the presence of spirit people fetching him and taking him from his body.

The last words he spoke were to tell her he loved her. Then he added, *'The only thing that is important is Love. Love is the only thing that matters.'*

She felt she was in his life to teach him how to express love. He was in hers to teach her to love and let go.

Linda's inner knowing that it was an agreement at soul level between her and her husband to be together for this short marriage, made the bereavement bearable.

Naturally, as a sensitive, loving soul, she felt the hurt and grief and loss but knowing the Truth helped her immeasurably. She could see the Light at the end of the tunnel. She could see the Purpose in the Plan.

Linda's clarity, her readiness to acknowledge her feelings and express them and at the same time to be aware of the Light were a real inspiration to me. I believe that Linda is lighting the way for others and shifting something in the collective unconscious beliefs about bereavement.

When a loved one is murdered, there must be a sense of violation, outrage and horror. And as with any bereavement, these feelings, as well as the rage and grief and pain have to acknowledged and expressed before they can disperse. And at the Spiritual level, murder is a contract between two souls.

At a soul level, no one can do anything to us without our permission.

I was watching television one night with my husband when there was a news flash about a particularly horrible accident in which many people were killed.

I said to my husband. 'Let's go to bed. I think we've got work to do tonight.'

Usually I bring no conscious memories of night work back with me, but on this occasion I took this teenager who had died in this particular accident and helped him to find his grandmother who had died some years before. She was waiting for him, knowing this was to happen.

As they saw each other there was a feeling of intense joy and delight, such as I have never before experienced at the re-union of two souls. I kept the feeling of intense joy with me throughout the next day.

So many things are different from the way they seem. I talked to a woman whose son was mentally ill. His life was becoming more and more severely restricted and he was living most of the time in a mental hospital. His mother took him to a well known and respected medium, who looked at his akashic records. She told him that he had undertaken to carry a gigantic slice out of the collective karma of mankind during his lifetime. He had sacrificed his life to help everyone. This was a choice at soul level and therefore nothing could be done to help his condition. When I find myself judging another I only have to think of this man and I suspend judgement!

Just as there are huge thoughtforms in the collective unconscious, there are family miasms,　great karmic blobs of negativity which hang over a family.

I feel that some of these are being cleared now. It often seems that one person in the family undertakes the collective karma of the family. In the cases I have come across the person who offers himself or herself is a really evolved soul. How else could they undertake so much?

Merina was one of six children. Her mother was powerful, dominant and mad. Her father was weak and ineffectual. Merina was the target of her mother's madness. The mother abused and tortured the child in horrific ways while the father was unable to support the child in any way.

As an adult Merina had undergone extensive therapy. She was also aware of her karmic reasons for choosing this mother. The whole family had a history of violence and madness, reincarnating again and again together, only to perpetrate similar horrors on each other.

When she came to me we worked through the emotional horror and hatred and reached the spiritual levels of understanding on many issues. At last the moment came when she looked into her mother's eyes. At first she could only see fear, which a reflection of her own fear. Then with a gasp, she became aware of the flicker of Light in her mother's eyes. The Light grew and she looked into the Divine centre of her mother's soul.

That was the moment when she began to dissolve the sticky spider's web of karma which held this family in its grip.

At the centre of every soul is Divine Light.

TWENTY-ONE

Birth Choices

Our inner personalities start showing themselves at birth or even before. Many a mother has felt an angry or agitated baby drumming his heels in the womb!

I was talking to someone recently who helped her granddaughter into this world by giving her daughter aromatherapy massage during her labour, relaxing her between contractions. All the nurses commented how serene the baby was when she was born. How wonderful to feel you are being physically welcomed into life, with such love.

When we choose our life circumstances, we choose our birth according to what we need to experience. The baby makes the choice of delivery with the mother's agreement.

By this I mean the incoming soul chooses the passage of birth with the agreement of the mother's Higher Self.

The mother is the baby's chosen vehicle into life and it is her responsibility to put her vehicle in order, mentally, emotionally, physically and spiritually to give the incoming soul the best possible preparation for Earth School.

Many souls who are reluctant to come into this life manifest this by putting the poor mother through a long labour. And many a mother who, at a soul level, is reluctant to re-experience a life with the soul who is entering, can put the baby through a difficult time.

All the careful preparation in the world won't stop a caesarean if that's what the baby needed to experience.

It seems we often choose to enter a life as we left another one in order to complete unfinished business. So if we die by knife, we may enter by caesarian. If we die by hanging, we may choose to have the umbilical cord round our neck, if we die by being trampled we may be born black and blue with a difficult birth struggle.

I particularly remember one workshop. One of the participants spontaneously regressed to her birth by caesarian. As that incoming baby she was so angry that I asked her to go back to her death in her previous incarnation. To her horror she found herself as a man being knifed to death in an ally. She felt betrayed and angry and cheated.

She brought a belief in betrayal and a feeling of being cheated with her into this life – and lots of anger and sense of struggle. She also told me that she has always been afraid of knives in a quite irrational way.

After the regression, the fear of knives has disappeared, but her belief in betrayal keeps her constantly in crisis. She needs to create a quiet space to start dealing with her deeply entrenched beliefs.

People who have recurring dreams about knives are often re-living old traumas of caesarean birth and past life deaths. The link between our chosen time in the womb, our birth experience and how we live our lives seems remarkably consistent.

Brian was a violently angry young man. He had an enormous death wish. He didn't know what stopped him from committing suicide. It was a daily option and way out. The thought of suicide was his escape hatch.

Brian was in his mid twenties and he had recently plucked up courage to take a job away from home. It hadn't worked out. When he returned home three weeks later, his sister had moved into his room and a lodger into hers. Brian had to sleep on the sitting room floor. 'There's no room for me,' he muttered through tight teeth.

During one session he re-experienced being in the womb. He felt only terror. He didn't want to be born, he couldn't go back and there was no room for him in the womb. Because there was no more room for him in the womb he was forced out into life.

As a child he felt there was no room for him in his parents' lives. They physically lived in a caravan so small that there was no room for him. His mother forced him to play outside. And now there was no bedroom for him. He continued to live out his belief.

We are so powerful that we can make others treat us as we believe we deserve to be treated. If we want to be treated differently it is our responsibility to change our beliefs.

I was musing about babies who choose to be premature when the phone rang. It was Pattie, a client whom I hadn't seen for many months. She told me that she had started to watch a programme on television on female circumcision. As she watched she felt so ill that she had almost passed out and she was sure it was important to explore this.

When she arrived for her session Pattie started talking about her aunt who was extremely ill with multiple sclerosis. She told me story after story about the way her doctor and even the hospitals had been treating her paralysed and pain ridden aunt. They appeared to be treating her with total lack of care, even callousness. Pattie was clearly upset and angry about this inhuman treatment.

I have long since learnt that when someone makes an appointment to deal with something and then talks passionately about something else, either the two are linked or the new subject must be dealt with first. I wondered if Pattie's aunt was involved in Pattie's story. As soon as I asked her to close her eyes and go back to the feeling she had had when she saw the programme on female circumcision, Pattie found herself as a five year old Indian girl in another life.

An Indian lady was mixing something red in a clay pot. 'She's bad. She does bad things. I don't like her,' the five year old child was shrivelling back into the chair with fear as she watched herself being placed on a couch.

Her mother, who was also her mother in this life was holding her down by the ankles as the 'bad' lady prepared to operate on the child's clitoris. Knife in hand she approached the child.

Pattie, as the Indian child, writhed with pain. Her face

was contorted with agony. At last she was still. 'I've got a purple light in my head. They're taking me out of my body. I don't want to come back.'

She was out of her body and looking down at the scene below her. 'My mother's frightened. She's shaking me. I don't want to come back.'

Her body began trembling in the chair as at last she came back in. 'I'm ill for a long time. My tummy hurts. I'm thirsty . . . so thirsty. I've a fever.'

Her mother and sister looked after her. Her father was devastated and very angry with his wife that she had taken the girl child to be circumcised.

Pattie kept repeating in her bewildered five year old voice. 'I don't understand. I don't understand.'

She died feeling angry and bewildered. From the state after death she looked down at the whole experience with horror, revulsion and disbelief.

I guided her back into that life to express to her mother and 'the bad lady' all the rage and sense of violation that she hadn't been able to at the time. This time when she passed through the moment of death, she felt much better.

Now she recognised that the 'bad lady' who did the circumcision, out of motives of power, was her aunt in this life. In a flash she realised just how much anger and hate that 'bad lady' had felt and held on to in her lives. She perceived too that her aunt's heart had light in it and she felt a flood of knowingness.

'My task is to send her healing and love. I want to hold her and cuddle her.' She allowed herself to hold and cuddle her aunt for some time – feeling warm and loving towards her. It was wonderful to see the transformation in Pattie. All the hurt and rage and fear had softened.

I wondered if her aunt was dealing with karma through her illness and attracting bad treatment from the medical profession, such as she had meted out in other lives. I'd like to feel that Pattie's compassion dissolved a whole lot of her aunt's karma as well as her own.

As Pattie and I talked about her experience, she realised that she had been born prematurely, nearly dying at birth because her mother had toxaemia.

Now she was aware that she had chosen that birth, possibly to help deal with the unfinished feelings of that Indian life – and of course at a higher level her mother had offered her body and allowed herself to become toxic so that Pattie could experience the birth she needed.

When my eldest daughter was born, I had toxaemia. She was born prematurely in Holland and spent several weeks in an incubator. In another life I sacrificed her as a baby and, in an attempt to expatiate, I offered myself for her to experience the birth she needed. She and I have all sorts of karmic ties, some good, some bad, offering many karmic threads to deal with and many opportunities for growth. At the same time I know she is a beautiful soul and I love her dearly.

It is interesting that she went back to live in Holland, the country of her birth, when she got her first job. We have both had lives together in Holland in the past. We all keep going back to places and situations in our efforts to learn our lessons.

Our birth story is often a metaphor for how we live our lives. Babies who come slowly and reluctantly are often slow and reluctant to do what they need to do in life. Those who felt they needed more time continue to have the feeling they are being hurried.

If we precipitate ourselves into life we usually rush and strive, and if we were stuck we often feel stuck in life.

The Universe has very clever ways of bringing these life positions to our notice.

A friend had been working on her stuck feeling. She was driving along a motorway in the middle lane. The slow and fast lanes were stationary and the middle lane was moving slowly. A car rushed up behind her flashing its lights and sounding its horn. She felt total panic. She was moving as fast as possible. Now she was being pushed from behind and there was no where else to go.

She found herself saying, 'Don't push me. Don't push me,' and realized this was an expression she often used.

As she realised the analogy with the birth trauma she

had been working on, she stopped panicking. She became aware that she was being presented yet again with important information. She decided it was appropriate to do some re-birthing sessions to help release unconsciously held messages which were no longer serving her.

The Universe helped with its usual synchronicity. As I wrote this chapter three people talked to me about breech births. The first told me that she was always scared of narrow waterways, especially with lock gates. If ever she was walking on a towpath she wanted to turn and go back as soon as she saw the lock gates.

She told me she had just had a dream of walking down a canal in the direction of the water flow. 'The gates are open and the water levelling and I walk to the final lock gate. There are other people there but I feel terrible fear and turn and go back. Two kind men come to fetch me. The father takes my right hand and the son takes my left hand.' Then I woke up feeling frightened.

As that incoming baby she felt that she changed her mind and turned to go back but it was too late.

What about babies who are born late? Either they are reluctant to come in or not ready to.

Betty was born a month late. She never got on with her parents. Her father said he only had children to look after him in his old age. She felt unwanted and sensed her parents never understood her or responded to her. Not surprisingly she was reluctant to come into this life to parents who couldn't understand or respond to her, so she hung on as long as possible and even then had to be induced. She realised she had been reluctant to deal with life ever since.

We may be reluctant to come in even though we have chosen balanced happy parents and an interesting life. The memory of Light is always more appealing.

People often ask me why they could choose to be adopted. It is not always easy or even possible to know why a soul makes a particular choice.

I know a gifted medium and healer who was adopted. Her adoptive parents were solid and sober and didn't appear to understand their imaginative, sensitive daughter. For years she felt misunderstood and angry. As an adult she traced her natural mother and found she was a way out psychic who couldn't cope with life. Her natural brother was in a mental home.

She realised then the wisdom of the social worker who placed her with a solid, unimaginative family. (This had, of course, to happen with the agreement of her Higher Self.) She became a balanced person who could use her mediumship and healing power and remain grounded. That just wouldn't have been possible with her birth parents.

Many souls make pre-life choices to be adopted because they need to experience a lifetime with no genetic blood ties – only spiritual bondings. It is not always an easy choice.

A young man told me that he chose to be adopted because he needed to learn that Love is Love and that regardless of parentage, there is only Love.

TWENTY-TWO

The Veil is Thin

The incoming soul chooses its name vibration with guidance before it enters. Then he imparts his name vibration telepathically to his parents. Usually the parents are listening all right, though sometimes one is more tuned in than the other. Occasionally parents choose a name but when the child is born and they hold him they just 'know' he should be called something else.

If the parents refuse to listen to the baby's telepathic message, the child may always feel at odds with his name and may change it later.

My first child miscarried very early in pregnancy, long before its sex was known. I had decided if I had a boy its name would be Russell. I had two daughters and when my son was born, I knew he wasn't a Russell, so we called him Justin.

When I moved into New Age awareness and started meeting mediums, psychics and spiritual people, I was told many times I had a son in spirit, so I realised that the baby who miscarried would have been a boy. But it wasn't until I meditated one day and felt his presence, that I asked his name. 'Russell,' immediately came to me. Of course! I should have realised.

I believe it helps many people with the grieving process, whether the soul has been aborted, miscarried, died at birth or after a few days, to recognise the baby's name and acknowledge it.

When we repress the grief, we keep it within us buried and it often emerges inappropriately or intensifies the feelings of a subsequent bereavement. All bereavement is cumulative unless dealt with.

Men especially don't know that they are allowed to have feelings about abortions, miscarriages and stillbirths. Often they just report tiredness or gloom and, of course, they can't support their partner in her feelings if they can't acknowledge their own.

Diana couldn't get over a bereavement which had taken place some years before. When she talked about her life, I learned she had had a miscarriage and stillborn twins, before her live children were born. These bereavements were barely acknowledged and rarely talked about.

She realised that she didn't know how the bodies were dealt with, what was written on the certificates or even if there were birth or death certificates for the twins. Her husband had dealt with it all and she hadn't liked to ask him.

Now, twentyfour years later, she was dealing with the buried feelings. She talked to her husband, and asked the hospital what the procedure would have been to deal with the babies' bodies. Even knowing something unpleasant is infinitely better than not knowing.

When she tuned into the twins to ask them their names, she received them straight away – Amy and Emily – and her face lit up. She and her husband bought a frame with spaces for family photos and put a photo of everyone in it, then wrote the twins' names in two empty spaces. This really acknowledged them. I have no doubt that Amy and Emily in spirit felt the linking, the closeness and acknowledgement and were happier too.

Diana asked me to use her real name and the twins' real names so that at last they would really feel acknowledged.

If we have a child who is aborted, miscarries, is stillborn or dies young, he continues to grow up in spirit with us. Of course, spirit children don't have a physical body, but if they show themselves to us, we usually see them at the age they would have been if they had lived.

I gave a talk one evening on dreams in which I explained how we make soul contacts with our loved ones during sleep. These meetings are sometimes remembered by us as dreams. Very often, if a loved one has died, we dream particularly vividly about them because we really are with them during our sleep state.

After this particular talk person after person shared how they had had visits during dreams from friends and relatives who had passed over. At the end someone came up to me shyly. 'I can't tell you how much your talk has helped me,' she said. 'My little granddaughter was a cot death seven years ago. We have never got over it and it's been a terrible grief for all of us.'

Then she told me that for years she'd had a very vivid dream of a little girl running up to her with her arms open. 'The child used to be quite small. I dreamt about her last week. She was about seven years old. She looked so beautiful and happy. I never realised until tonight who the child in my dream was.

Children in spirit love ceremonies and being acknowledged. I put a bauble on the Christmas tree for Russell and for the other children in spirit that I know.

I am sure they return the love we send them. One night I was very deeply asleep and a long way from my body. My husband was in India on a business trip and due back in the early morning. However his flight was early.

I dreamed that three children were knocking and knocking at my bedroom door. I got out of bed and opened the door. They told me I must get up. I recognised them as spirit children and thanked them and let them out of the front door, giving them a little present as they went.

Still in a 'dream', I went back to bed. Then I woke up.

My husband arrived home ten minutes later. He was three hours early and I was awake and ready to welcome him. If the spirit children hadn't come and fetched me back gently from where I was, I could have had a nasty jolt trying to get back so quickly into my body.

Babies, born and not yet born, can influence their parents' behaviour. Tammy was a psychic sensitive and very mediumistic. She had chosen a life in which she experienced much sexual and physical abuse.

Tammy's father was having an affair with another woman while her mother was pregnant with her. When her mother told her father she was in labour and asked him to come to the hospital with her, he refused. He spent the night with his mistress instead. So Tammy was neither welcomed nor greeted by her father.

Her father continued to live with her mother but Tammy never felt he was interested in her and he died when she was a child.

Tammy came to see me feeling very angry. She had contacted a memory of her father touching her genitals on several occasions when she was a toddler. She had a real feeling of sexual violation.

As she told me of these memories and feelings which had come up, she slipped automatically into a past life experience where her father was her trusted older brother. When she was fifteen this adored and trusted brother and confidant started abusing her. He continually raped her. She was hurt, bewildered and had no one to turn to.

She screamed out in rage and impotence as these memories surfaced. For some time she vented her feelings and then I helped her to raise her energy to her heart centre and be totally aware that she was a being of love.

She saw herself sitting in the barn where her brother usually raped her – only now she was experiencing unconditional love energy. She felt and knew at once that he had no need to touch her sexually any more. They sat together with a sense of oneness. There was no need to forgive. It was all dissolved as if the violation had never been.

We moved forward to the time when she was in the womb waiting to be re-born. She was carrying the old memory of anger and violation and she saw how her father had telepathically picked up her rage and hadn't wanted to greet her at birth.

She then connected with herself as the toddler being sexually abused. In a flash she became aware that he had split up with his mistress and felt sexually powerless. He mistook sex for power and wanted to have power over his family.

Raising her energy to her heart centre, she was again aware that he had no need to touch her sexually when she radiated unconditional love energy. It was only when she activated her old anger and impotence that he connected with her on that level.

She realised that even in the womb she had set off the rejection by her father and later sent him the messages which allowed him to violate her as a toddler. Now she was able to find a oneness with him at the heart level.

Tammy started a process of consciousness change so that she knew she need never again attract a man who would violate her.

When we take responsibility, we accept that we, the incoming soul, influenced our parents to behave to us as they did. This brings us release, growth and freedom.

Sometimes, when a soul is reluctant to come into life, he will make attempts to go Home during childhood.

These are the awarenesses that Mavis made about her childhood longing to go home.

She attended a workshop I was running where we drew maps of our bodies. I commented on a scar she had drawn on her throat. She told me she had always had throat problems and tonsillitis. At the age of three she had her tonsils out but during the operation, she had opened her eyes. This had so shaken the surgeon that his knife had slipped and damaged her throat. A little of her tonsil had been left in her throat and she had had recurring problems.

On another occasion she had had the awareness that as a baby she hadn't wanted to be born . . . and when she had been born she didn't want to stay. The doctors had said she was too sickly to live, but somehow she had held on.

She came for a session to do some more work on her awareness round her throat problems. She relaxed and slipped back into her childhood and found herself at three years old running home from playschool to go to hospital to have her tonsils out.

'How do you feel?' I enquired, expecting her to say she felt frightened or reluctant. I was quite surprised when she said, 'Happy.'

'Happy?' I echoed. 'Yes, I'm happy. This is the end. I won't be coming back. I can go back to the happy place where I was before.'

I moved her forward to the operation and she saw her body on the operating table. She was out of her body, above the operating table, willing the surgeon to make a slip with his knife and release her.

From out of her body, she focused on her physical body on the table and forced her physical eyes to open so that it would startle the surgeon. As this happened and his hand slipped, she turned to leave for the Light. But there was no Light. There were only helpers coming to tell her it was not time and that she must face the future.

She became red in the face with anger and frustration because she couldn't go. And her wise Guardian in spirit came to the child and explained why she must stay.

'I hear what he's saying and I'm nodding to agree . . . but I'm going to try again to leave as soon as I can,' she said, in her three year old voice.

As her adult self she told me that she stopped breathing when she was five and had emergency resuscitation. Later still, when she was twenty, she was due to go on a coach trip. At the last minute something stopped her going and another person took her place. The coach crashed. Her replacement died. She still wasn't released to go Home!

Now I asked her as a three year old what she needed to enable her to face her chosen life, with purpose. Immediately her Guardian took her to show her good times in the future. She still wasn't convinced that was enough to make her want to live.

I suggested she ask to be allowed to see the tapestry of her lifetimes, past and future, to understand why this was so necessary. She saw Beings rolling out the tapestry with the past and future coloured in. This life was a blank.

She started to laugh as she realised she couldn't reach the future without living this life. Seeing the bright colours of her future lives, she felt the reluctance to live slipping off her like a cloak.

TWENTY-THREE

The Doorway of Death

Just as we choose our birth, so we choose our death. We choose the way we go through the doorway to the next room we have to explore on our journey.

One person chooses to die quietly in bed. Another decides to be ill or fade away over a few weeks, possibly to give his family a chance to get used to the loss.

Another may live flamboyantly and decide to go as he lived, in a very dramatic way.

Most of us have read of masters who tell others that they intend to die at a specific time. They prepare themselves and withdraw their spirit from their body at that time. The only difference is that this is done consciously and most of us don't bring our choices of death to consciousness.

Sometimes we hold on for a reason. For instance a mother may wait until her daughter arrives from the other end of the world, to say goodbye and then die.

There are some people who hang on because they are attached to people and don't want to let go. Their loved ones may also be hanging onto them and prevent them from going to where they should be.

If someone we know is dying, the greatest gift we can offer him is to make sure we are not holding onto him.

A man came to me and explained that his mother was dying. He loved her dearly as did the whole family and he felt they must be holding onto her. He didn't want to be responsible for keeping her when it was her time to go.

I asked him to close his eyes and visualise his mother. Then he saw himself and his brothers and sisters. He saw a cord going from each of them to his mother, holding her back. He had a sense that these cords were restraining ropes stopping her from leaving. With love and reverence, he cut his cord to her, and told her from his heart that he loved her and was ready to release her. He prayed that the others who were holding onto her would be helped to let go.

Later he told me that a shift took place in the attitude of the family that day and within a week, the old lady had been freed to go on her journey.

It can happen the other way round. Someone who has died may be hanging onto someone in life and influencing them badly. A young man, who was a client of mine, was haunted by his mother when she died. The mother came to him in dreams every night to exhort him to keep everything as it was. He also felt her angry presence everywhere he went.

His parents had split up, the husband leaving his wife for another woman, and his mother had never forgiven his father. She died embittered and determined that the other woman would never be accepted.

The young man was paralysed at work, socially and in his relationship with his father because of his mother's refusal to let go. He loved his father and would have liked to meet his new wife but he didn't dare to do anything against his powerfully influencing dead mother.

I consulted a friend of mine who is a very powerful medium, to intercede with the mother, to persuade her to pass on and leave her son to lead his own life. But my friend told me it was a very strong karmic issue between mother and son and she didn't want to let go.

So I worked for months with the young man, strengthening him, helping him to see that the Truth is always love and hanging on is fear, helping him to see the relationship with his mother and father in a new perspective. Very gradually the mother's influence weakened.

We also knew from the dreams he reported that his mother, in spirit, was also healing as he healed. At last she moved on to the next stage of her journey and no longer haunted her son. He was free to love her and equally love his father and stepmother. Now she came back to visit him in dreams with messages of love. And on special occasions he felt her presence as a warm loving feeling.

Sometimes we keep people artificially alive on life support when their spirit has left the body. I do feel this is a contravention of spiritual law. Even though the silver cord attaching the spirit to the body has severed, so that the person is spiritually free of his body, very few souls can leave their physical bodies lying in a hospital bed for weeks, months or years without being constantly drawn back to look at it.

Euthanasia is often discussed. If someone kills his dying parent because he wants to save him or her pain or indignity, as he perceives it, the intention is what is taken into account. If the act was done with selfless motives, then there is no karma.

However, very often we learn our most important lessons in our last weeks, days, hours or even minutes before death. The moment of death is often the moment of greatest illumination.

So when he reviews his life and realizes that he prevented his dying parent from having an important learning, he will want to help her to learn that lesson on another occasion.

When people are holding onto material possessions they may become earth bound after death, not really understanding that they are dead. This is a very unhappy state to be in, which is why ghosts are generally sad.

Some people work as rescue mediums, helping to persuade such unhappy souls to pass over properly. Few of us realise that there are many who do similar work and are quite oblivious of it because they do it in their sleep. We are in earth school twenty four hours a day. Often our sleep time is our most hardworking time!

A young man phoned me up because he couldn't wake up in the morning. My guidance told me that he was working very hard during his sleep state helping souls to pass over. This was soon after the earthquake in Armenia when many souls who died were in shock and disorientated and needed help to pass over. I was told to tell him this so that he would understand the reason for his problem.

When he arrived for his appointment, he was a burly young builder, just about the last person I would give such a message to. I wrestled with my guiding voice throughout the session.

'Tell him he has been working in Armenia every night,' my guidance insisted. 'Tell him that was why he was ill before Christmas.'

I kept frantically sending back the thought. 'No I can't possibly do that.'

Finally I succumbed. I asked him if he had been ill just before Christmas and to my relief, he confirmed that he had had pneumonia. So I explained to him that we all work during our sleep time. We leave our bodies and do various things. I told him that he had been working in Armenia helping earthquake victims to pass over, some of whom were deeply in shock and resisting. I told him he had been ill before Christmas because he had been overdoing it on the inner planes.

He listened intently to all I said. Then he said, 'Oh my Mum was told she helps souls to pass over. I never realized I was doing it too!'

After that he just needed two sessions to impress upon his subconscious to take him for healing before he returned to his body and to return in good time for him to get up for work in the morning. He had no more trouble with getting up.

Yet another lesson for me in trusting my guidance!

And a lesson to so many of us to stop being so hard on ourselves. There are times when we wake up exhausted in the morning and we may have been doing a very hard night's work. There are times when some of us go a very long way out of the body to Halls of Learning where we are being taught something very important and we have travelled so far in different vibratory levels we can hardly wake up.

As I was thinking about this chapter I kept hearing about suicides. All my life I thought suicide was a cop out, an unwillingness to do what we came to do. It generally is just that and the life has to be re-done.

However, the Universe has a way of drawing aware-nesses to our attention. Within the space of a few months, three different friends said this to me about three different suicides.

A young man hanged himself in a friend of mine's garden. She had known him and his family for some years. She was a medium, so I asked her why he committed suicide. Her response startled me. 'He'd completed what he needed to do in this life and this was his way off the planet.'

Some time later I was talking to another friend, also a medium about her friend's suicide. Again I asked why. Her response was similar. 'At some level he realised he was recalled – maybe not consciously, but he heard the call and responded.'

The third friend I asked about yet another suicide quite simply said this, 'He knew it was his time and left'.

At the same time most people who commit suicide do so because they feel they can't cope any longer. When they do pass over there is no punishment. They receive healing and love before they return.

The only punishment that there is is the awfulness of watching the effect of their suicide on their loved ones. Often they watch their partner struggling to bring up small children alone, confused and hurt by their defection, or elderly parents blaming themselves and stricken by guilt and grief for their adult child's untimely death.

A friend of mind who sought help about a member of her family who committed suicide, was told that he was in deep sleep, receiving healing and being gently watched over. She was assured that when he woke he would be surrounded by souls who loved him, so that he could learn to open up to love again.

For many people the grief at the death of a loved one is compounded by the belief he died in pain. And there are endless instances where loved ones have come back, through dreams, through mediums or directly to the bereaved person to say that their death only looked painful. They felt nothing.

Because we have seen the body contorting with agony, we presume the person is feeling it. Usually the spirit has left the body, and the physical body is responding automatically but feels nothing as consciousness is with the spirit.

One mother was worried about what it felt like for her son when he was killed in a head on car crash. She kept replaying it in her mind. But he came through to her very quickly and told her that others may have seen a car coming towards him but he only saw a ball of Light.

There are many reports on the between-life state. It seems that, if we need healing, either because of our emotional state or because of a physical illness, then our spirit goes somewhere where we can be nurtured and healed. Healings take place with colour rays and loving thought vibrations.

We meet our loved ones, though not with physicality. That is no longer necessary. And the negative emotional bondings have dissolved so we are able to experience truly loving relationships.

We can also see people as they really are without the limitations of their human beliefs, so we can see that grumpy hurtful neighbour as a being of joy and the painridden, angry relative as a healthy being, radiating love.

There is no physical speech, of course. In higher vibrations communication is telepathic. This means total honesty. To think is to communicate. It is the same with movement. To think yourself somewhere is to be there.

We can serve in other realms as we can here. We can learn and we can teach. We may refine a lesson to bring it back to Earth on our next visit. We may be privileged to guide someone who is on the Earth plane. And we continue to move into higher and higher planes as we become ready, refining our vibrations and becoming lighter.

Some years ago I went for a walk with a friend who is a really old soul, the only volunteer I have met in the flesh. That means she did not have to return to Earth. She volunteered to come back solely to help others.

She asked me what I intended to do when I passed over. I replied that I hadn't given it a thought. She said that she had asked to work part time welcoming to the other side new born babies who had died, and helping them to understand their lessons.

When we pass through the doorway of death into the summerlands and then into higher planes, we experience vibrations of love and compassion we have no concept of. The colours, perfumes and the music are such that we cannot imagine them. There is much to look forward to.

It is no wonder that those who have experienced a near death experience and seen the Light lose all fear of death. They then know death is a doorway into a new life.

TWENTY-FOUR

Transformation Time

We are one. If the waters of the ocean evaporate and fall all over the earth as rain, each droplet is the same essence as the ocean from which it originated. Each droplet will in some way find its way back there.

And in the same way we are all part of the divine Source spread over the Earth. We are all the same divine essence as each other and the Source. It is time now to recognise this oneness.

In the Aquarian Age grace will dissolve karma so that we can all live in oneness. In the New Age we will live in harmony, equality and love with each other. We will serve nature and live in harmony with the natural world.

When we feel the stirrings of spirit within us, it is time to listen. Then we will hear the clarion call from the Highest and we must respond with our all.

It is at this time now that the calls are going out to individuals to aim for the Light.

Our true self is immortal, timeless and eternal. Now we are asked to heed the call and reach higher, reach above the personality self to the all wise, all forgiving, part of our being.

The aim is that we become so attuned to our Source that God and man will work together and co-create a world of love, abundance and delight.

During the transition we must accept that everything is just and perfect. The Spiritual Laws put everything right. God has infinite ways of balancing all things.

So accept now that if some people have fallen into a pit, it is a complete waste of time and energy to get into the pit and suffer with them. It is pointless to sit at the top of the pit and commiserate. It is senseless to pull them out if they are going to jump back in.

Our task is to go within, into our deep inner wisdom and ask if there is something for us to do. If the answer is, 'Yes' then we must act to get them out with as much energy as if they were our own children.

If the answer is 'No' then we must honour our fellow men and respect their right to stay stuck or grow in their own way.

What we can do is radiate Light onto the situation. When we do this, every cell in our body opens and pours out divine energy. Our aura becomes bright and luminous and this Light touches the hearts and minds of the people involved. We are doing more good than we have any concept of.

And when we are open and radiating, the Higher Powers see our Light. By the quality of our Light they know that we are ready to be used. Then they can pour their higher energy through us to touch people and situations and work miracles.

In the Universe at this time there are seed thoughts, seeds of new ideas and concepts, and wonderful energies, lying waiting for us to reach out and draw them in to use them for the good of mankind.

New ideas and inventions have always waited in the Universe to be picked up by anyone who is ready. As ideas have become available, people have reached for them. This is why inventions and discoveries are made in different part of the world at the same time. And people call it co-incidence!

However, at this time there are greater seed thoughts than ever before waiting to be picked up. There are incredible, wonderful energies waiting for us. As more and more of us become ready to reach up and draw them in, it will help to raise us into realms of consciousness and awareness that we can't yet conceive.

So let us forget our ego, our personality, our pettiness

and differences and allow our spiritual self to shine beautiful and luminous. We only have to send thoughts out like antennae towards these great new energies and invite them into our being. Everything responds to thoughts. These new energies of Love and Light must then enter us and start their work. They will lift us higher.

The Earth plane has been in darkness far too long. Now walls are tumbling down, individual ones and physical ones. Dictatorships are falling as we claim our power.

As the Light intensifies, it focuses on our darkness within. This can no longer be contained and conflicts ensue and continue where we cannot raise our vibrations. We are told there will be chaos and disaster and confusion in the times ahead as many are creating massive dramas in their efforts to reach the Light.

And those who are beacons stand strong and steady amidst the chaos and confusion, secure in the Truth.

Many who are not ready for the higher vibrations of the New Times will pass over. And so many will leave the planet.

Some who are ready will choose to pass over to help in spirit from the other side. Never say that someone has died, therefore they were not ready for the New Age. They may have wonderful work which calls them over.

We must simply concentrate on raising our own Light.

This is a time for Transformation. It is time to clear our Path to the Source. All are being invited now to change and raise themselves.

Those who are attracted to read this book and similar books which are being spread now from the Source are called to prepare themselves to lead the Earth through this time. It is an honour and privilege to heal and lead and inspire others.

We must not waste energy wondering if our desire to heal and teach is from our ego. We must get on with it.

We are called on now to be beacons of Light and to light the way for others.